Seven Letters
from Patmos

Ruth Aird

Also by Ruth Aird

History: Revealing Your Genesis
(A series of short meditations)

Letters to Jennifer:
An audio presentation of our Heavenly Fathers plan
in giving present hope for an eternal future

The seven letters that our Lord sent to the churches of Asia at the time of the Apostle John, dealt with problems which were both relevant and serious. If our Lord's message was needed and necessary almost 2,000 years ago, equally, and perhaps more so it is vitally required for the good of this generation of believers. Ruth has presented these timeless truths in a way which is both readable and relevant. I thoroughly commend this book.

Eric Scott, Carrubers Christian Fellowship, Edinburgh

This powerful book brings to life the Book of Revelation in a very challenging way. It is a comprehensive description of John's exile to the Isle of Patmos, where God gives him a word for each of the seven churches in Turkey. I believe that the way this book is written gives a very strong "wake-up " call to the church today. Take heed brothers and sisters!

Fiona Castle OBE

Letters from Patmos effectively combines and integrates the factual basis of John's final years on Patmos and his erudition, with a carefully thought through theological interpretation of the first three chapters of Revelation.

Gordon Dutton Emeritus Professor of Visual Science Glasgow Caledonian University

The seriousness and determinacy with which the author lays down the basics of all Christian faith is overwhelming. The reader is enabled to understand intricate texts and bridge the gap between far away times and today. That is so important in terms of Biblical texts, otherwise people will not understand why they should spend their time reading the Bible. This is not a dry retelling of what we can read anyway anywhere but an enlivening that makes you hold on to your breath. Yes, it DOES matter whether you are a Christian or not and YES, it must show in your life, otherwise it is of no use and a bland name tag to your life.

Suzanne E. Lier Author of the family storybook Journey Through the Old Testament (vol. I and II) with Masterpieces of Art, Auditor University of Bonn

'Seven Letters from Patmos' is an absolute tour de force: engaging... accessible... creative... informative... serious... stimulating... thought-provoking.

Jim Grover, Photographer

This book shows that Revelation is not just a book of the past but one for now, today. The history is used to challenge our failings as followers of Christ; otherwise it would be meaningless. 'Seven Letters' is encouragement that is exhortation. Not to be merely read, this is a book that should make you stand up and act.

Miriam Montgomery Co-Ordinator Free Church books, Scotland

Choklakas Bay, Patmos

Seven Letters from Patmos

Ruth Aird

Beithe Publishing

2020 Beithe Publishing

Seven Letters from Patmos

Copyright 2020 Ruth Aird

Requests for information should be directed to ruth@reaird.plus.com

Cover Image: First panel of Threads 'First and Final' through Revelation by kind permission of Jacqui Parkinson www.revelation-threads.co.uk

All photographic illustrations belong to Ruth and David Aird

All scripture quotations are taken from the New International Version of the Bible 1984 International Bible Society.

Logos drawn by Alan McKay

Maps are provided by Biblos Maps http://bibleatlas.org

A record of this book is available from the British Library

ISBN: 978-1-8381181-0-5

Beithe Publishing
13 Mauricewood Bank
Penicuik
EH26 0BS

Printed in Great Britain by Bell and Bain Ltd, Glasgow

Front cover First panel of Threads 'First and Final' through Revelation by kind permission of Jacqui Parkinson www.revelation-threads.co.uk

For

David

Emily and MaryBeth

Seven Letters from Patmos

The Revelation from John the Apostle was sent by letter to the seven Churches in Asia, from a tiny island in the Greek Dodecanese which lie off the western shore of Turkey. At the end of the first century AD the last book of the Bible as we know it was about to be written.

Caves on the north side of Patmos

Contents

Page

FOREWORD

I first met Ruth Aird through her work on local Christian radio in Scotland. That connection then deepened when I began to visit Golgota Bible School in Talamciu, Romania, a place that Ruth and her husband David have been involved with for a number of years. It is a joy for me to call her a sister in Christ and to admire the energy and dedication that she and David devote to serving the Lord. It really is a privilege and pleasure to have been invited to write the foreword to this fascinating book.

 I challenge you to join Ruth Aird on this compelling journey through the letters to the seven churches of Revelation. You will be transported back to the Christian communities who first received these letters and helped to see these texts through their eyes. The Book of Revelation unfolds the incredible purpose of God for the future; it is a book about looking forward. However, Ruth reminds us that the first readers of Revelation were real communities of real believers in real places. A rich and vivid picture is painted of the cities where these early Christians lived and worshipped. Yet, this book is not an historical textbook. Ruth takes the crucial further step of asking each of us not only to look forward and to look backward in history, but to look inward. The journey of this book is one on which you will have to stop often to reflect on the deeply personal challenges each letter presents. This process is particularly encouraged by the helpful questions Ruth has included at the close of each chapter. These questions, as well as being useful pointers for individual reflection, make this book an invaluable resource for Bible study or discussion groups. The first four words of the Book of Revelation remind us of its central focus, *'The revelation of Jesus Christ'*. At the heart of 'Letters to Patmos' is not its first readers or even ourselves, but the glorious person of Jesus Christ.

Indeed, this book serves as a vital reminder that when we read Revelation and consider the future events John describes, we are dealing not with theory, nor fantasy, but reality. This book will help you to look forward to these events, backwards in history and inwards in personal reflection. Ultimately however, the impression left with you when you have finished the final page is a desire to look upward, as we *'wait for his Son from heaven'*.

Iain Jamieson
Evangelist and Preacher

INTRODUCTION

'No eye has seen, no ear has heard,
no mind has conceived what God has prepared for those who love
him, but God has revealed it to us by his Spirit.'
1 Corinthians 2:9, 10

Picture an enormous painting of images previously never seen, filling a room, walls, ceilings, and floor. If twenty people lined up to enter that room and each was allowed ten minutes (equivalent to our lifetime in terms of world history) each would come out of that room with their own interpretation of that picture. To take in the whole canvas, kaleidoscope of colours and tumbling images would be so overwhelming that some would concentrate on one square foot; others would look at the colours; the imagery; a single concept or perhaps a whole wall for an overview. The narrative of the picture would be determined by the understanding, world view, traditions, and culture with which they had stepped inside the room. Each interpretation would have an individual resonance in all probability inexplicable to one another.

Imagine then, that canvas is the visual narrative of Revelation. Images never seen before crowd in upon you, yet occasionally catching a glimpse of something you once had seen or known years before. Just as in that room of crowded paintings, there are as many different understandings of the book of Revelation which can overwhelm our logical thinking.

What happens when we look at this book as the culmination of world history finishing with a glorious new heaven and new earth? The Bible is the living Word of God who created us in His image, gradually revealing Himself first to individuals and then to the nation of Israel. The pattern of worship given to Moses in the desert is continued through the generations until finally He introduces the world to His Son and writes the rescue plan for his lost and straying children. As Jesus rises from the dead and ascends into heaven the watching disciples are told that this is not the end of the story, in fact it is a new beginning. They are to go out to the ends of the earth and invite all nations into God's kingdom.

The last book of the Bible is a plea from our Lord Jesus Christ to remind all the churches that bear His name to be serious about their witness in the communities where they live. To show the urgency of this message, John is given a vision of the last days on earth. Revelation was not written in isolation by a man in a cave on an island. Instead, John's images were based upon those given by prophets such as Isaiah, Daniel, and Ezekiel, filling the gaps as he was shown by his guide through the age to come. Jesus when on earth had also given John material to use as he wrote down the vision that he saw while in the Spirit.

Revelation, says John Stott, 'lifts the curtain which hides the unseen world of spiritual reality and shows us what is going on behind the scenes.' God is working his purposes out in ways we cannot understand with finite minds therefore Revelation cannot be read like an ordinary book. It lives and moves in directions previously unknown without any chronological order following no earthly structure of writing. It points backwards to the beginning of time, and forwards to a time known only to God. It is set in the vast halls of eternity which have neither entrance nor exit and we have no world view which can make sense of the detail.

Many people do not want to read Revelation for it troubles and annoys them. They cannot see what John saw and are often dismayed at a world they do not want to know and cannot imagine in their present comfort and ease. Perhaps most of all it causes them to fear the image of an awesome God, for whom it is a sin to disbelieve and who stands in judgement on those who will not believe in His Son. The Lord said to John and others on many occasions 'Do not be afraid.' We are not to be afraid but rather know that perfect love casts out all fear. That perfect love is God Himself, preparing for us who believe an eternal home without pain or sorrow, a place where He can once again live with us.

What you are about to read is a gathering together of jigsaw pieces from an array of experiences traversing continents, eras, and lifetimes. Each piece is like a nugget of gold that comes out of Havilah where the gold of that land is good (Genesis 2:12). A friend once remarked that it is essentially a book about the revelation of the Lord Jesus Christ – revealing him in all his glory to every person who has the courage to read it. Its message is that Jesus Christ has defeated satan and will one day destroy him altogether (Stott, 1986).

As I am sitting writing this a chaffinch has just flown into the window of the sitting room. There was an explosive noise as the tiny bird hit the window and fell into the leaves, lying there gasping for breath. It believed it could fly where it wanted to, and so at full flight it hit a barrier it had not seen. A bird has no understanding of the barriers presented by a manmade fiber. But we as humans have been given instructions and understanding as to how to live our lives from the source of truth in God's word. Yet somehow, we miss that truth. We fly at full pelt through our lives into glass and fall back wondering where we went wrong. Yet still God strives to bring us the truth, pleading with us to listen to what he is saying before it is too late. Sadly, for my little chaffinch it was too late, and his demise will feed the pine marten family in the grand circle of life. Revelation is a book of warning with dire consequences if not heeded.

This book is written as a narrative of the first three chapters of Revelation, so if you want an interpretation of the Book of Revelation you can visit the references at the end of the book. Amongst these are the ministers, apologetics and interpreters of the Word of God, people who are true students of the inspired word of God. I would encourage you to read what they have to say but always return to the Bible, asking the Holy Spirit to take you on the most awesome journey of your life. Catherine of Siena who died tragically at the age of thirty-three, said that 'all the way to heaven is heaven' (Sherrill 2002).

One of the most inspired books I have read on Revelation is the journey of Jaqui Parkinson (2016) who sewed a visual representation of John's vision onto twelve banners. Her book simply and honestly maps out her own view of Revelation in the light of extensive research, asking the reader to be stirred by the Holy Spirit to think about the deep *'issues of life and faith – death and judgement – hell and eternity – and the New Heaven and New Earth'* (p20). Once you have read God's revelation, you will never be the same again for your journey will become to you the most inspiring and joyful travel opportunity that you will ever have. From beginning to end it is the story of the one true God, revealing himself to mankind who consistently and doggedly tries to run away from the one and only truth. Place yourself in God's guiding hands and enjoy the journey as He shows you the untrammeled beauty of His story to woo mankind. A story that culminates in this book of Revelation which is still to come.

The photographs in this book are living proof of the island of Patmos. It is a place of quiet serenity, where inspiration blossoms from seeds deep within the heart and the words from John's pen find soul filled expression. On holiday in Patmos I felt the presence of John arriving on that little island in the autumn of his years looking back across his life. No words could do justice to the visions that John saw whilst on the island. But through faith, as you read the Book of Revelation which has come straight from the mouth of God, you can feel and know His awesome and holy presence. You may experience the wonders of the Lion of Judah, killed at the hands of violent men and let tears slide down your cheeks as you see him triumph in heaven having purchased men, women and children from every tribe and language and people and nation with his own blood.

Revelation was written for Christians then and now, to give them an understanding of the hope they have in the future of this world and a sight of the marriage of Jesus and His bride the church. To read this account as an unbeliever in God would either cause panic and fear or a sense of nonsense and foolishness. Paul said in his letter to the Corinthians (1 Cor 1:18) that those who refuse to believe the message of the gospel see it as stupidity, while to believers it is the power of God. As believers in the Holy God we have faith in His plan, and we trust His promises. Those promises from Genesis to Revelation not only include everlasting life, but also judgement for those who do not believe. This then is the crux of the matter and the reason for anger on the part of unbelievers at the temerity of anyone who would try to show them the future. The picture of judgement is too close for comfort, when deep within their consciences they recognise that the way they are living is not the standard God has set in His Word.

The glorious truth of Revelation is that it gives encouragement for the present as we endeavor to share the gospel with those who call us foolish. It shows a picture of an absolute and holy righteous God, who has spent all the time the world has had to show us His love and asks us to turn to Him in repentance believing in His Son Jesus Christ. We catch glimpses of that perfect purity within which there must be judgement for those who choose not to be made pure. Above all we see our Saviour, still bearing the marks of His death as He beckons us to spend eternity with Him in a place that He has been preparing. Nothing could surely give more pleasure when we as believers, read these words.

Finally, (Rev 1:11) John is given a command to write down what he saw and send it to seven specific churches. From there it would go viral across all nations and tribes, generations, and eras of time. At the end of his vision John was told under no circumstances was he to seal up the vision, instead he was to go public with it. Times had changed since the days of Daniel who was given the same prophecy and told to 'seal it up until the times of the end' (Daniel 12: 4). This is now the 'time of the end', where Jesus says that soon the Son of Man will be seen coming in clouds with great power and glory (Mark 13:26). Right now there is a window of opportunity, for those who do not yet believe to repent of their ways and return to the Lord. John, Daniel, Ezekiel and Isaiah fell in the presence of the one true God as their knees could not hold them up. They recognized His awesome and fearful authority over death and hell and above all His perfect holiness. May we recognise the awful yet joyful certainty of revealed truths in Revelation and go on bended knees to the only One who can and does rescue us.

Ruth Aird June 2020

Patmos, East end May 2014

CHAPTER ONE

'In the beginning was the Word, and the Word was with God'
John 1:1

Dialogue between the Apostle John and the Roman Governor of Ephesus written *by the late Burns Shearer, Scottish Fellowship of Christian Writers*

A Matter of Appropriate Communication

Prosecutor: Are you John, son of Zebedee, sometime of Galilee and now of Patmos?

Witness: Yes.

Prosecutor: You are a fisherman?

Witness: Yes.

Prosecutor: And do you have a brother James?

Witness: No sir.

Prosecutor:(Accusingly) No?

Witness: I did have a brother James, sir but he is ....no longer alive.

Prosecutor: And were you and your brother James part of a gang, a group of radical revolutionaries based in Judea and Israel?

Witness: I am a disciple of my Lord, Yeshua of Nazareth along with my brother James.

Prosecutor: Insurgents, am I correct?

Witness: No sir.

Prosecutor: You planned and conspired to bring about insurrection.

Witness: No sir. We wanted merely to change men's understanding

Prosecutor: I warn you not to try the patience of this court.

Witness: What I have said is true. There was no planning of insurrection.

Prosecutor: I must remind you; you are under oath. I shall ask you once more. Were you a member of a gang or cell of revolutionary intent on undermining the authority of Caesar?

Witness: We did not plan or take part in any form of insurrection against the authority of the Roman Empire or the Tetrarch in Jerusalem or even the Jewish Sanhedrin.

Prosecutor: I put it to you that under the leadership of this Yeshua of Nazareth, you, your brother James and the others were part and parcel of an underground movement which sought by covert and clandestine means to foment revolution among the common people and to subvert the authority of the government. Is that not the case?

Witness: No sir. With respect, I think there has been a corruption of communication. Our Lord's teaching was to render unto Caesar, the things that are Caesar's

Prosecutor: You constantly refer to him as "my Lord". What exactly was the nature of the authority this Yeshua that you speak of was seeking?

Witness: He did not seek it.

Prosecutor: What do you mean?

Witness: He already had it.

Prosecutor: (Scornfully) He already had authority?

Witness: Yes sir. His Kingdom is not of this world.

Prosecutor: (Puzzled) Is not of this world?

Witness: No sir. My Lord sought only to save men's immortal souls from the penalty of death. He made no claim on any other territory.

Prosecutor: Do you have any proof of what you say?

Witness: Yes.

Prosecutor: What possible proof can there be that this man Yeshua is who he claimed to be?

Witness: His resurrection from the dead.

Prosecutor: He rose from death to being alive again?

Witness: Yes.

Prosecutor: There are witnesses to this?

Witness: Yes sir. I am one.

Prosecutor: You expect this court to believe you?

Witness: I pray that everyone who hears of My Lord truly believes what I have seen with my own eyes.

Prosecutor: Then that would have to be a matter of appropriate communication?

Witness: Yes sir, it is very much a question of communication of Good News. In the Greek tongue, what is known as 'The Gospel'.

Prosecutor: (Thoughtfully)You are the most unusual fisherman I have ever met. In this case I am not going to press for the death penalty. Instead, I will seek to have you put to work in the salt mines here in Patmos. You and your testimony will either be destined for oblivion or, if not, well, let's just leave it there shall we?

The Pathway up to Hora from the bay in Patmos

Chapter Two

He (Jesus) was with God in the beginning. Through him all things were made; without him nothing was made that has been made.'
John 1: 2, 3

John arrives on the Island of Patmos

After a long sea voyage from the seaport of Ephesus the apostle John arrived on the island of Patmos. Around 90 – 95 AD the Roman Emperor Domitian had decreed that John should be sent into exile on the island that the Romans used as a place of imprisonment – a remote and inhospitable place, where few people lived – a tiny backwater of the Roman world. On the way from Ephesus where he had been living for the past few years John must have had many thoughts. He was around 80 years of age and half a century earlier had been a young Jewish man with a future in front of him – learning all he could from the Rabbis at synagogue school; going into his father's fishing business; marrying the girl his parents chose for him and then having children of his own. A smile of hindsight must have played around his face as he looked across the sea to the small island of Patmos which was to be his home – until the Lord returned. For wasn't that what Jesus had told him: to remain as a witness until the gospel had been preached all over the world (Acts 1:8).

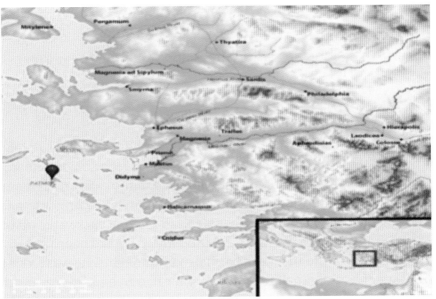

Biblios maps

He had been loaded unceremoniously onto a commercial ship which Romans used to ferry their prisoners around the East end of the Mediterranean. He thought of Paul, so often a guest of these prison ships, kept away from prying eyes down in the galleys, where men were used as rowing machines when sails lost wind.

He did not know the future, but he knew his Lord. This was the one whose shoulder he had leaned upon during that very last supper they had together before he was taken and murdered. The one whom he had seen wrapped in linen cloths, certified dead by a Roman soldier and then three days later, realising with sudden clarity that Jesus was no longer dead but alive and was indeed the Son of God. How did they not see it all those years they were with him – the tears pricked his eyes as he thought of their mistakes and lack of understanding. Since the day Jesus had disappeared out of their sight, so much had happened. Thousands of people across many countries had come to have a living and personal relationship with the Son of God. It had been phenomenal. Miracles of healing both physical and emotional added to the amazing conversion of one of the most vociferous Christian haters. Paul had advanced the gospel further into Europe than it would ever have gone without him. His brow furrowed as he thought of the torture and martyrdom of many of his friends, fellow brothers, and sisters in Christ. Oh the sadness of losing his fellow disciples. Of them all, he was the only one left. Yet even the horror of their martyrdom could not dim the pride he felt at their commitment to the gospel of Jesus Christ. They had followed Him to the very end and given their lives for Him just as He had said.

His eyes blurred again as he remembered his brother James, the first apostle to be martyred, beheaded by Herod to be popular with the people (Acts 12:2). In fact, that was when Peter narrowly escaped being killed having been arrested during the Feast of Unleavened bread and imprisoned. How amazing that the prayers of those early Christians had been answered when his chains were broken by an angel and he was led through the streets to his friends in the middle of the night. He had certainly seen many stories like that happening for real. Time and again he had proved the power of the Lord Jesus Christ, both in his own life and in that of others. His brother had had a knack of drawing alongside people to tell them about Jesus, but his pride had caused him to learn a hard lesson at the feet of Jesus. John grimaced as he thought about this. It was not only his brother that had learnt that lesson. He too had learnt that Jesus was not just a human friend – he was the Son of God. While both he and his brother were in training as apostles, though they did not realise it at the time, their mother had asked Jesus if James and John could sit one on either side of Jesus in heaven. He squirmed with embarrassment – not at his mother, but at his own pride in thinking that she was right to ask. How needless that now seemed for it was never about being famous or powerful. Jesus was teaching them that it was the least who were called into his kingdom. Those who were at the bottom of the social structure and who knew they were worthless, understood that they were sinners. The lesson of servanthood was for all, no matter how high or low they were in society.

'I have set you an example, said Jesus, that you should do as I have done for you. I tell you the truth, no servant is greater than his master, nor is a messenger greater than the one who sent him.' John 13: 15,16

Yes, sighed John to himself, there is sin in every man, woman, and child – but they must see it for themselves. His dear brother, the first to be killed by men who thought they could get rid of God, had been so busy passing on the words of Jesus. Despite his death the Good News had ricocheted around the Mediterranean for it seemed nothing could stop the word of the one true God. He remembered dear Gamaliel who so wisely spoke words which were surely from God (Acts 5: 38). *'If their purpose or activity is of human origin, it will fail. But if it is from God, you will not be able to stop these men; you will only find yourselves fighting against God.'* And fail it had not, for this was of God's purpose. He instinctively looked up, *'The first shall be last James,'* he whispered, *'it will not be long before I see you and our beloved Saviour will be there crowned with glory and honour.'*

As the little boat neared the barren island with barely any flat roofs to be seen, John wondered what he was to do there for his Lord. There was no doubt in his mind that he had been brought for a purpose. He tried to remember the words he had written down all those years ago – his memory was not as quick as it had been, although the joy in his heart was quicker than ever to respond to the Holy Spirit's nudging. It was something like: *'He cuts off every branch in me that bears no fruit' (John 15:2)* and certainly over the years he had been pruned. 'I thought I could be the greatest, the first in fact, after all I was his best friend. But Jesus loved us all equally. Peter was to be the leader, not me. I am the servant of God: when I get pen and paper on the island I must write that down (Rev 1: 1-2). What else did Jesus tell me?'

'Every branch that bears fruit he prunes so that it will be even more fruitful.' Behind his beard was a toothless grin. In those heady days when the Holy Spirit fell on all of them, he realised with clarity that Jesus had indeed been pruning them. It was to prepare them for that time when so many people kept coming to belief in the Lord. Disillusioned with their false religions and the emptiness of their lives they saw a joy and peace in the disciples that they didn't see in their religious leaders. People started calling them apostles, so in fact they all became leaders in one way or another. They led people to this new way of living that was sacrificial yet caused previous sworn enemies to love one another; to give up their possessions and share them with each other; to live without anxiety or cares and instead live in peace.

'No branch can bear fruit by itself' (John 15:4). He had written down those words with the Holy Spirit breathing on his pen and fanning those words into flames. Looking back he saw the necessity of living life embedded in his Saviour, Master and Lord. Of course, he could do nothing without Jesus and could not think of bearing fruit without his Lord as Master. As John realised the message of love that God had been sending the world since before the beginning of time, his mind and pulse raced! He loves us so much that He is continually sending us messages and His Son was the culmination of that love. Am I here, he wondered, to be the voice of hope to a desolate volcanic piece of rock in the middle of the sea? Or perhaps, he mused, I am here to listen to another love letter from my Saviour.

The boat slid in through a narrow gap of rock in this practically deserted place. A natural harbour had formed behind the gap where the water was calm. The hills rose around him, green and lush in the Dodecanese climate. A strange rock formation rose in the centre of the bay as if God were saying to him: 'Remember John, it is on this rock [meaning Christ] that I shall build my Church' (Matt 16: 18). Peter had been given that place of leadership amongst the apostles in Jesus' physical absence, but not the leadership of the whole church – no, that had been solidly placed in the hands of their Lord now seated at the right hand of God. Instinctively John raised his eyes heavenward, 'O for a glimpse of my King in glory,' he breathed. 'Perhaps here in this beautiful solitary place I will be given that glimpse.'

CHAPTER THREE

'In him (Jesus) was life, and that life was the light of men. The light shines in the darkness, but the darkness has not understood it.' John 1: 4, 5

John settles on the Island of Patmos

The Bay of Grikos, Patmos

The boat crunched suddenly on a pebble bed jerking to a stop before reversing with the motion of the sea. Momentarily John was transported to that time on the beach where he and the other disciples had breakfast with the Lord (John 21:12). Peter had leapt out of the boat leaving the rest of them to pull it ashore full of an unaccountable catch of fish. 'Come and have breakfast' Jesus cried, as if it were the most natural thing in the world that He, the risen Christ, was their chef for the morning. Yet there He was providing for their daily needs, cold starving fishermen needing the comfort, warmth, and love of a heavenly father. He had never ceased to provide for all their needs, through all the tragedy of martyrdom, persecution, and governmental tyranny he never left them on their own.

With failing body parts as he started what must surely be the last part of his life on earth, John reached out his hands to those who offered theirs and half stepped, half fell onto the beach in this small fishing cove. Ragged children stood watching this rare sight of a visitor landing on their island. Men put down their nets and women waited. Roman soldiers were to be feared, but this was different. Why bring an old man under guard to this forgotten place? Patmos was an unknown jewel in the east of the Mediterranean, with a closely guarded extensive array of fruit, vegetables, oils and honey that few knew existed.

Yet here in their midst came a man who seemed to hold an aura of peace around him, with a deeply infectious smile. The soldiers stood around – no-one had told them what to do once they arrived with their prisoner and the captain of the small boat that carried them across was agitating to return. They had embarked on the last leg of their journey as soon as light had broken and were fearful of navigating hidden rocks in these uncharted waters as darkness fell.

Bay on the North side of Patmos

A woman broke free from the watching knot of people. 'We have little,' she said, 'but what we have we will share with you, old man.'

He looked at her face, smiling slowly, 'and I too have little but will share with you a miracle,' he said.

So, John the apostle arrived in Patmos, far away from the noise of city life and the stress of wondering who was going to knock at his door. For some reason, the governor of Ephesus had decreed that he should not be killed as all his companions had – perhaps one more martyr would further a cause the Romans wished to die a natural death. So he was delivered into the hands of a community that enveloped him, came to know and eventually love him. His name lives on today on plaques and buildings in surprising places unheeded by tourists.

The soldiers gratefully returned to the boat, pushed out to sea and John set his face inland to the next chapter God had written for him, the one whom Jesus loved, to share what he had been given.

Over the next days, weeks and months John told his story to the villagers, but it was not his story. Instead it was the gospel of peace, in the words that Paul wrote to the Romans (10: 12,13):

'there is no difference between Jew and Gentile – the same Lord is Lord of all and richly blesses all who call on him, for, everyone who calls on the name of the Lord will be saved.'

Every day the villagers would gather and listen to this ancient man tell the stories of Jesus and of his love which compelled him to perform miracles for ordinary people – just like them. They came to believe in one who had died for them, whose blood was spilt in a perfect sacrifice for their sins. They believed John when he told them how he had stooped in through the door of the tomb and saw only grave clothes. They never tired of listening to the story of Jesus appearing in the room where John was with the other disciples and telling them to look at the nail marks on his hands and feet and the deep scar in his side.

John taught the younger men how to read and write, feeling instinctively that he needed to pass on all those stories even on this little island.

The villagers cared for this elderly gentleman, seeing him as holy, someone who was like the one he called Jesus, of whom he talked about all the time. They gave him somewhere to live, somewhere to teach the youngsters – they were proud of John the Teacher.

But often John would escape – away up to a cave on the side of a hill. He furrowed his own pathway up to a niche in the rock and whenever the villagers saw him pick up his staff they knew they were to ask no more questions that day. 'He needs time with God, so he can tell us more,' they would whisper to one another. And there in the cave, John would sit, kneel, or lie flat on the floor, seeking counsel from his heavenly Father. He prayed with tears for those he had left behind, for the Christians across Italy, Spain and as far as the newly emerging countries in the western reaches of the Roman Empire. Always he would return to the village with his face shining and his eyes bright with a burning passion to tell more to the people who lived under the shadow of the acropolis their ancestors had built, to whom they sacrificed in the hope that their lives might be protected. But they were learning a different way.

Monastery at Hora, the capital of Patmos

Today, looking up at Hora, the capital town of Patmos, with a total island population of 3,000 people, a bulky brown stone building sits atop the crest of the hill like a bird's nest. It fills the skyline commanding an awesome presence. Priest-like figures move around it dressed in conventional black or grey and the blue sky softens the iron fist of locked church doors. Across on the next hill lie the ruins of the previous dynasty, an acropolis with a dead investment of religious fervour that did not last. In Athens, a similar investment lies in ruins – another acropolis being restored so that tourist worship can continue – until the finite heap of stones collapse once again. In our modern society the pantheons have similar shapes - pillars and rectangles with altars of extreme sensitivity, known as the mobile phone. They know you and your income, your bank balance, your likes, and dislikes. Our worship of gods takes place 24/7 and from any place we happen to be for we carry the altar of retail with us wherever we go.

Yet if visiting tourists would care to look beyond the religious trappings they might just see the peace they seek in the legacy that John left behind. A book called The Revelation of John the Apostle of Jesus Christ, written and published by the one and only true God.

Chapter Four

The true light that gives light to every man was coming into the world. He was in the world, and though the world was made through him, the world did not recognise him. John 1: 9, 10

On the Lord's Day

Each Lord's Day, the first day of the week, it was John's practice to climb the hill behind the village to his cave, taking with him a flagon of wine and a loaf of bread in a leather bag slung over his shoulder. He would slowly tread the path with worn leather sandals and a branch from a sturdy tree secure in his hand, his staff to comfort him.

The pathway from Scala in the bay to Hora, the capital city in Patmos

Often on his solitary walks John would think back to the early days when all the disciples were on fire for the Lord – he would never forget the sight of three thousand men, women and children queuing to be baptized that very first Pentecost. They had used as many house pools as they could to try and baptize all the people that kept coming. The laughter and the joy that was present in Jerusalem that day was unforgettable, for the people could not keep the smile off their faces as their heavy load of sin was taken away from them by believing in the risen Christ. And then as the fire of the Holy Spirit took hold of everyone, they were all desperate to get back to their home countries and tell everyone about Jesus. The disciples themselves wanted to travel telling as many nations as they could that Jesus was alive and would save people from their sins if only they would call upon his name. John himself had travelled right up into Turkey preaching as he went.

Paul was the most travelled of all of them, even although he was not in the original group of disciples. But no–one was jealous, it was pure joy listening to each other preach supporting and encouraging one another. Although he had not been there in Athens, he could picture the many scenes that Luke had written about as Paul and the others spoke on top of the hill they called Mars at the Areopagus. It looked out across Hephaistos; the temple dedicated to yet another stone-faced god. Little was John to know that with the passage of twenty centuries those temples would be roofless, filled with tourists come to be entertained. God or gods meaning nothing and all the same.

The bustling thoroughfare of the Athenian Agora was a hotbed of disputes and discussions for all travelers who would listen to anyone with a story – this was Paul's territory. Speeches were timed with a clay klepsydra, a water clock. Marble ballot boxes and descriptions of ostracism bore testament to the apparent civilisation on which Athens was built – no city was as fine as this one. Decrees of the Assembly of Demes ousted tyranny, despite the cruel dictatorship of a long line of Caesars who saw their god like existences as necessary to the civilised world. The Panthenaic Way stretched through the centre of Athens like a snake wriggling up to the masterpiece which stood atop the flat rock of the Parthenon itself. The Patelic marble shone in the sun as the Athenian worshippers flocked to revel in the classical civilisation of the Greek world that would surely never end.

Would it end one day, John wondered? Would the line of the great Caesars one day only be a line in the history books and the great acropolis be left to slowly recede back to the earth from which the stones had been taken? What would remain? As he turned it over in his mind he thought of the scribe that he had been teaching to write and he knew what would remain. The one and only true word of God. No matter how many Christians were martyred; no matter how hard dictators tried to take believers out of the world or destroy the manuscripts that had been copied a thousand times over, God's word was written on people's hearts and would be whispered wherever there was an opportunity. Jesus had said that even if no one would talk about the majesty of his Father, the stones would eventually cry out. Nothing and no one would stop the march of the soldiers of Christ across the world and down through however many ages it took for Christ to return.

The Parthenon, Athens

Here he was then in Patmos on the first day of the week which was the day the Lord had asked each of them to remember until he came back again. John went back to the last Passover meal and played over the scene in his mind – the table laden with roasted lamb, unleavened bread, the bitter herbs of horse radish, parsley in salt water and the sweet mixture of raisins, grated apple, honey and almonds. Then, just before the meal was served, Jesus washed their feet – John's eyes always filled with tears with this memory – the Son of God washing his dirty feet! How could he have let Him? But in those days, he felt he was important amongst the rest of the team. Jesus took a loaf of bread and broke off a piece for each of them – this represented His body which He gave them. After this, Jesus passed around a cup of red wine and told them to take a drink each because this was a picture of His blood being poured out for them as a new promise. Remember me, just like this, He had said – so they had, every week on the first day of the week, they remembered Him and taught all new believers to do the same – always until He comes back, they told them (Luke 22: 19,20).

What a privilege it is to remember our Lord Jesus Christ at the beginning of every week in the same simple way that he asked the disciples – with bread and wine. In the presence of such a sublime holy God, how dare we omit this remembrance from our weekly diary? John and the rest of the disciples practiced this to their last days on this earth and taught all those believers who they were discipling to do the same – 'until he comes, until he returns' was the oft repeated refrain (1 Cor 11:26). Right in the beginning after Jesus had risen from the grave and returned to heaven, the disciples and new Christians met together in the temple courts and in their homes to break bread and remember his death and resurrection. As the narrative continues in Acts, a pattern develops in meeting regularly on the first day of the week (Acts 20:7). It was good practice for the Christians to meet on a set day particularly as whenever they travelled or were made refugees they would always know when to meet the Christians. Paul asks them to ensure that they made a collection on that first day (1 Cor 16:2) because that is when he knew they would be together. There is no mention that this is a command to meet on the first day, rather a plea from the Lord not to forget him (Luke 22: 19). If we love him, we will do as he asks and remember him with joy and thanksgiving.

No matter where we are in the world, no matter whether there are 2 or 202 of us, bread and wine are easily obtainable. There is no need for special words or ceremony, special clothing, or utensils. Just a desire to remember the Lord, his death and resurrection to remind ourselves once again of what we have been saved from. During the time He was in the tomb our Lord Jesus descended into the depths of a hell that was never meant for man, only for satan. As a sinless being he wrested the keys of death and hell from the devil who no longer had control over men and women who choose to believe in the saving power of the one who died for them (Rev. 1:18).

There is no need for any one of us to spend eternity in hell – we are all invited to the eternal reaches of an immortal life with the God who has given all He has in order that we might live with Him.

John had taught the villagers who believed his message to do this and they were glad to because they had the Holy Spirit in their hearts as a gift from God which prompted them to worship the risen Christ.

On this Lord's Day, the name the disciples had called the first day of the week, John climbed his path to the rocky outcrop which overhung a cliff edge on the hillside, and felt the Holy Spirit give his earthly spirit a peculiar lift. He stopped on the path and looked around him. The island smelt beautiful, with pinks and reds of blossoms bursting through dense scrub, birds calling to one another, goat bells clanging sending an echo from hill to hill. He held out his hand and an emerald butterfly landed on his palm, stretching out her wings to show a full circle of rainbow colours. Right in the centre for a second, he could see something – then it was gone, and the butterfly danced away on her journey to somewhere. He continued up the path as it twisted and turned through pine trees with the scent of rosemary bushes following him as his coat brushed the leaves.

Arriving at the cave, he took a long-handled broom from the back and swept it clean ready for his Lord. He set out the bread and wine on a rocky shelf and settled down beside it on his bag for a seat. His spirit continued to be strangely stirred, and he felt as he did the night of the last supper when he lent against the shoulder of his Lord. 'It was as if He were right here,' he thought as he looked expectantly around the cave. 'No, not His time yet,' he murmured to himself. Yet there was a feeling of expectation in his soul and he felt very close here on the mountainside in the thin air of this island of Patmos. He thanked God over and over for bringing him into this place of exile.

As he remembered these things his hand went out to the cup of wine, ready to identify himself with the blood of his Lord. And as he did so, reverberating around the cave came a voice that sounded like a trumpet call!

The voice which boomed across the cave, the valley, the hill and beyond was clear, every word spoken etched on John's brain.

'Write what you see and send it out', was the command. John already knew that his account of Jesus' life had been copied hundreds of times and probably more, so eager were the readers to replicate it.

He must have had the thought even then that these words held such importance that it would not stay with these churches alone. In those few moments, John realised why he had been sent to Patmos – here his earthly life was to end, but it was the start of something new for the whole Church of Christ. This was a revelation that was to give renewed hope to tortured, persecuted, and endangered Christians across the world.

Startled by the voice which sounded like a trumpet, John swiveled round to see where it was coming from and there in the corner of his cave of which he knew every nook and cranny he saw seven golden lamp stands. As his eyes adjusted to this uncommon sight he saw a figure standing amongst the lamp stands. He half started up as his first thought was that it was Jesus! But he knelt instead wondering with mouth open wide and no words – it was Him surely it was! Wasn't it? There was something so familiar, yet strangely different. His mind raced trying to take in the whole scene before him for the voice had told him to write down what he saw yet how could he describe what he saw? There were no words for the person who stood before him. He was like a man with clothes that resembled men's clothes – a robe with priestly vestments covering it. But there were parts that John could only describe as resembling a lamb – for the hair covering his head was like wool but startlingly bright and eyes that flashed fire deep inside them. He glanced down and saw that there were feet protruding from the bottom edge of the robe – but feet like he had never seen before. They were glowing a beautiful deep honey colour that bronze has when cleaned. Yet at the same time it was like looking straight into the blinding searing heat of a furnace for melting the bronze.

All the time, as this being spoke, the sound was just as if John were standing right underneath an immense waterfall. As his eyes travelled back up to the face of this Son of Man, yet not a man, John could only do one thing – he fell forward, knowing that he was a sinful man in the presence of the Holy God of all the earth.

Then, wonders of wonders! John felt the pressure of a hand he knew so well on his shoulder and the voice repeated words that John had heard many times during those three years as companion to his Lord

– 'Don't be afraid!'

Don't be afraid! What joy it was to hear those words remembering all the times they had meant so much to him personally as well as to the other disciples.

Out there on the lake of Galilee (Matt 14:27) they had seen a human being walking towards them through the gale force winds that were driving the little fishing boats away from home. At first, they had thought they were seeing things and then as they realised they could all see this human form they were terribly afraid. It was outside of the norm, totally and completely other worldly. The tangible relief they felt when they realised it was Jesus culminated in Peter jumping out onto the churning sea and walking by himself towards Jesus. If truth be told, John had rather wished he had been as impetuous but was glad he hadn't been when he saw Peter sink through the waves.

Then there was that glorious time when he realised that no longer was fear going to intimidate or identify him. Something happened that third day after Jesus was crucified and buried (John 20: 8). The women had been to the tomb and came back to say that someone had stolen His body. John would not have put it past the Romans to do something like that to discredit the testimony of Jesus, so he and Peter ran to the place where Jesus had been laid to rest. It was indeed just as the women had said – there was no body in the tomb. However, there was something else which changed John's life forever. All the strips of linen which had been wrapped around the body were lying in a separate place from a neatly folded burial cloth which had been wrapped around the head of Jesus. No grave robber and least of all the Romans who had no feelings for Jewish bodies, would have unwrapped the head garment and then folded it up nice and neatly separate from the rest of the burial cloths. On that Sunday morning, John lost his fearfulness and believed that Jesus had risen from the dead although he did not understand why. He had lost his fear until now that is, for this image that stood before John on the island of Patmos was more other worldly than John had ever experienced. Now the feeling was fear mixed with a joy that he could not articulate. The words spoken were sliding down a sharp double-edged sword and sounded like a mighty cataract.

The voice continued to tell John He was there from the beginning and would be there until the end. Even although John had seen Him alive, dead, and then alive again, He was now alive for ever, with the power to open the gates and place of the dead. The Lord explained the seven lamp stands as representative of seven named churches, and the stars, which John now noticed in his right hand, were angels, one for each of the churches. He started to dictate individual messages to each of the seven churches, hugging the western coastline of Turkey moving inland, forming a circular route. The churches were known to John although he had not visited them all, but he knew Christians there and had supported and encouraged them through letter writing, meeting some of the elders and full-time workers.

John listened with eager anticipation for the words that were going to challenge not only these churches but all the churches across the kingdom of God.

CHAPTER FIVE

'The Word became flesh and made his dwelling among us. We have seen his glory, the glory of the One and Only, who came from the father, full of grace and truth. John 1: 14

Letters to the Seven Churches

In the book of Revelation, John was given a series of letters to send to seven churches throughout the country of Turkey. Almost two thousand years later we have received those same letters and seven snapshots of what our world church is like today. We experience the same pattern of living that the churches had in Asia and the letters are for us to read and act upon (James 1: 22-25). John expected his readers to respond and engage with his writing personally and individually. No matter what age we live in and no matter where we are in our walk with God his message still applies. All seven letters speak of the conditions present in the church during this age of grace, that is, the time between Jesus dying on the cross and returning for a second time. They were written in order – the order that they were to be delivered following the major Roman road, which starts at Ephesus after arriving from Patmos and then north to Smyrna and Pergamum, turning inland to Thyatira and south to Sardis, Philadelphia, and Laodicea.

These are letters from the Lord Jesus Christ – our bridegroom in waiting, revealing the detail of the wedding feast that awaits us in heaven prepared by His Father. The first few letters give us an idea of the way in which he wants us to work together as churches while preparing ourselves for the wedding day (Rev 21:2). Read the letters as if you were reading them from your fiancée – the person with whom you are going to spend eternity. Personalize the words of the Lord Jesus and let them challenge your attitudes. Be excited, yet awestruck by the vision of God on the throne and His Son, the Lamb who gave His life for all people.

We have already been given a guarantee of our future eternity in Paul's letter to the Ephesians (1:13-14). During an eclipse of the moon across the sun, the moon sits perfectly over the sun forming what is called a 'diamond ring'. The darkness of the moon exaggerates the brilliance of the sun behind it and the ring of light bursts out in a perfect circle all around the sun. We are the bride of Christ, dark with sin yet made holy through the blood of the Lord Jesus enveloping us in his righteousness, shining so brilliantly that the light eclipses all our badness and ungodliness. The beloved in Song of Songs (1:5) described herself as 'dark but lovely' because her lover did not notice her unfashionable dark skin. Instead he loved her beyond her external features. In the same way, our Lord does not look at our dark features, whatever sin it is that has ravaged our bodies. The brilliance of our Saviour dispels all darkness and we are left bathing in the light of his love for us, that made him pay the price for our eternity, the ransom for which is priceless.

Just like that diamond ring in the eclipse we wear in our lives the 'engagement ring' of the Holy Spirit as a guarantee of the union that is to come in heaven of the Son of God and his bride, the Church. This wonderful picture of a wedding day in heaven allows us to look forward with anticipation and hope as we live in a world that is filled with pain and sorrow. Jesus used the wedding feast as a way of describing the kingdom of God that is being built on earth (Matt 22:1-14) and John the Baptist used the same simile to describe the joy he had in recognising Jesus as the bridegroom who is Christ (John 3:29).

While Revelation is filled with many images that are beyond our understanding and have been given many different interpretations, there is an unmistakable message to the church on earth. We are being watched over by a loving, but holy and majestic God, who holds the keys of death and hell through the Son who died but lives eternally. This is a message to say that we can totally rely on the Living One, but we must listen to what he has to say, not just with our ears but with our hearts and minds, ready to implement his desire for us.

Instructions for reading the following letters:

Each of the following letters are written in the same format so that you can follow them through with a structured plan if you are using this in a bible study. Each part is written in a different font so that you can follow the letter reading that font section. Or you can take each letter as it comes and read the whole, answering the reflective pieces at the end of the letters personally or in a group.

Summary

There is a very short summary in a box at the beginning which if you are short of time is all you need to read. However, if you want more you can go onto read the rest. With the summary is a logo for each church as an aide memoir.

John's memories of the Church

For some of the churches there is evidence that John either knew various members or had visited to support and encourage them in their witness. The gospel according to John and 1 John were both generic letters written to churches while John was still in Ephesus before being exiled to Patmos. 2 and 3 John were written to specific people in those churches but became part of his portfolio. His memories will have been acute as he realised the impact of what he was writing to people he knew well; people who he had mentored and prayed over with tears. He knew the cities they came from and their hopes and fears as they laboured for the Lord in these places. These were real places, real people, and although John did not know it the message was going to go viral long before social media was ever conceived.

The Letter

This is in italics from the New Living Translation. The message for the church follows in a letter format – perhaps written and assisted by a scribe or disciple, sent out by the next boat arriving many weeks later via the Roman road post to the addressee on the envelope. Imagine the excitement as the elders of the church received this precious parchment from the disciple of Jesus Christ who was their mentor and their beloved brother in Christ. I wonder what they thought John was going to say to them as they undid the parchment and laid it out flat on the table in front of them. A few words only, but a challenge for the whole church and not just in their small area of Turkey. Nor was it for their time only, it was for all churches who believe in the Lord Jesus Christ – his death and resurrection - and a call to rekindle the love for their Saviour that some of them had lost or exchanged for the lie of satan.

The History of the Church

After the letter follows a brief history of the city and surrounding areas. This is pertinent to the letter John wrote, for the Lord knew the influence that their surroundings had on the Christian values and witness of the church. Some of the churches had withstood this influence with remarkable courage and consequences, but others had been swept along thinking they were strong, so much so that there was no difference between the church and the world around them.

Message to the Church and application for today

Then there is the lesson of application. What do these letters mean to the church at the time and what is the relevance to us in the twenty first century? How do these words fit current lifestyles and what is the message to each individual person?

These letters come at the end of the Word of God. This living, active, sharper than a double-edged sword book of instructions (Hebrews 4:12) is not to be taken lightly. The message is for us all to thoroughly digest and meditate with a seriousness that will change our attitude and have everlasting consequences for our relationship with our heavenly Father.

Personal or group reflection

Finally, an instruction for us all, 'Whoever has ears, let them hear what the Spirit says to the churches.' We need to meditate on these letters, seeking God's will and the practical application that the Holy Spirit wants us to apply in our churches.

John's Church in Ephesus

Summary of the letter to the Church at Ephesus

Ephesus was the capital city of Roman Asia and the centre for worship of the goddess Diana.

The group of Christians there had flourished under Paul's teaching, working hard despite those who did not preach the truth. However, they had been so busy in doing good works that they had forgotten their love for the Lord. Instead all that they were doing was for their own gratification. The Lord pleaded with them to return to loving him as they did at first and to repent of their pride in what they were doing. It was not going to be easy to admit their failures, their spiritual pride and legalistic church procedures, but in doing so they would find joy as they looked forward to the reward of overcoming when they finished the journey in their eternal home.

There is a serious message to us all if we reject the pleas of our Lord Jesus to repent and return to our first love. If we ignore him then he will turn away from our churches and remove the witness that we once had in that community, giving it to another church. We cannot expect to have the privilege of witnessing for Christ and the blessings of the joy he gives us if we do not hold tightly to his word of truth.

Now read on...............

The Library at Ephesus

John's memories of the Church at Ephesus

As John heard the Lord say write to the angel of Ephesus he must have felt his stomach leap. Although the Bible does not place John in Ephesus there is evidence from other writings (Tertullian and Irenaeus) to place him in this city for some considerable time. John must have thought a lot about Ephesus – particularly the time he had spent there with Mary the mother of Jesus. It is presumed that Mary was with him until her death as Jesus had asked John to look after her knowing the persecution that would follow his death and resurrection. They were precious years and he had listened again and again as Mary retold the miraculous story of the birth of Jesus – the poor innkeeper; the shepherds; the wise men; Anna the old woman in the temple and Simeon. The house was always crowded because so many people wanted to hear her stories. It was her story, yet at the same time it wasn't, for she was telling the narrative of the Son of God. The awe in her voice told the listeners that this was no ordinary story for it held the answers for all mankind if they could only believe it. The understanding came not before the believing but afterwards. How beautiful it was to see people's faces as they believed in the Son of God, and then the rapture which shone through their eyes as they understood the love of the God of heaven for them personally. Paul brought Priscilla and Aquila to the church in the early years (Acts 18:19) and although he only stayed for a short time on that first visit he was persuaded to return. It was this godly couple who had been the mainstay of the Ephesian church with their hospitality and desire to disciple new Christians like Apollos from Alexandria (Acts 18:26).

The Letter to the Church at Ephesus

Ephesus, thought John, my home, the place from where I was forcibly removed and exiled to this lonely but beautiful jewel of an island. The place where the Lord knew I was going to write a letter and send to all the Christians from whom I was exiled! I am looking now in your direction across a sea which only separates our bodies. I am bound to you in spirit and I love you all, my brothers, and sisters.

Rev 2: 1-7 (NLT)

Write this letter to the angel of the church in Ephesus.

'This is the message from the one who holds the seven stars in his right hand, the one who walks among the seven gold lampstands:

I know all the things you do. I have seen your hard work and your patient endurance. I know you do not tolerate evil people. You have examined the claims of those who say they are apostles but are not. You have discovered they are liars. You have patiently suffered for me without quitting.

But I have this complaint against you. You do not love me or each other as you did at first! Look how far you have fallen! Turn back to me and do the works you did at first. If you do not repent, I will come and remove your lampstand from its place among the churches. But this is in your favour: You hate the evil deeds of the Nicolaitans, just as I do.

Anyone with ears to hear must listen to the Spirit and understand what he is saying to the churches. To everyone who is victorious I will give fruit from the tree of life in the paradise of God.'

I love each one of you in our Lord Jesus Christ,

Your own

John.

History of the City and Church at Ephesus

Ephesus was previously a Greek colony and was at the time this letter was written, the capital city of Roman Asia (Asia Minor) and a centre for land and sea trade. The headquarters of the goddess Artemis (Diana to the Romans) was the origin of a vast array of iconic industry dedicated to her name. Her sacred month was May – exactly the time when Paul, preaching in Ephesus, was dragged into the theatre to answer the silversmiths. The guild of silversmiths in Ephesus was a union strong enough to influence the whole city, until Paul's teaching reduced the sales of silver models of Artemis and portable models of the temple. These were mummy shaped bodies with many breasts, the head of a female with a mural crown and a bar of metal in each hand. The temple of the great Artemis, who was reputed to have fallen from heaven to earth, was one of the 7 wonders of the ancient world, with 120 columns six feet in diameter and sixty feet in height – now only a single pillar left in a field of coarse overgrown grass where people walk their dogs. Ephesus was notorious for magical arts and amulets of parchment inscribed with incantations.

It was these parchments, with a total value of around 50,000 pieces of silver, that were burnt in the public marketplace by confessing Christians, no small thing to burn (Acts 19:19). In fact, this incident sparked a revival amongst those Christians who had been afraid to openly confess their faith and with their confessions, many others believed. The church in Ephesus was, at this point, spiritually strong in their love of the Lord and desire to serve Him and Paul left the church in good hands. Paul placed young Timothy there as pastor sending him many letters of support and encouragement, which he needed to weather the criticism and challenges that faced him in the church. In the letter to the Ephesians we see that Timothy's teaching had indeed been diligent but challenging and although heeded at the time by some members there was evidence of issues that were not being addressed (Eph 4:17–32).

Paul himself tried to warn the elders of the church in Ephesus (Acts 20:29) to be on their guard, for 'savage wolves' would try and eat away at the solid base they had established. He reminded them of the hard-grafting work he had done to supply both his own needs and that of others and to exemplify this in their lives. Ironically, it was exactly these works of service that the Ephesian church was to turn into a form of legalism causing what Lotz (1997) calls the 'delusion of service.' Paul's letter to Timothy (1 Tim 1:3) brought this legalism and false doctrinal teaching to everyone's notice – Timothy needed to be strong and while John may have been there some of the time, he would not always have been able to support him in person. There were others who were strong in the faith and stood with Timothy such as Onesiphorus and his household (2 Tim 1: 16) and Tychicus (2 Tim 4:12). This was the church at Ephesus – strong on the outside with many good men teaching God's word, but at the same time trying to ward off those who would destroy the work of the Holy Spirit and their first love for Jesus.

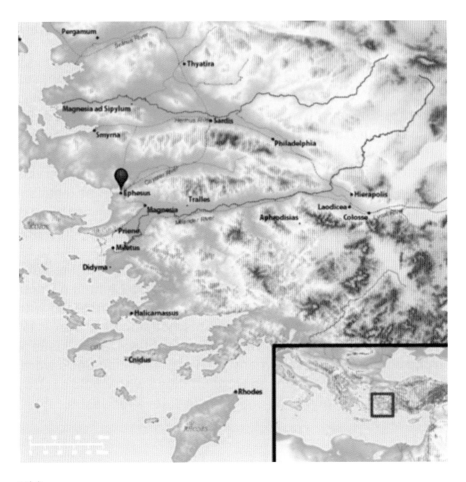

Biblios maps

Message to the Ephesian Church and application

Ephesus means desirable – a true description of Christ's church in the seaport on the western shore of present day Turkey, now some five miles inland from the coast. A church that Christ desired as a part of his bride.

The Lord pointed out three main areas of Christian living to His desirable church:

1. Identity – the Lord knew each member intimately in that church; what they were like; what they were capable of and how much they had already endured for His sake.

2. Passion slippage – the Lord saw beyond the veneer of their outward appearance, detecting spiritual arrogance and a turning to moral righteousness within the community rather than serving out of love for Christ. Their original passion had given way to a legalistic form of service and they were focusing on that more than on the person of the Lord Jesus Christ.

3. Eternal life – the wonderful reward of living a Christ filled life is to eat from the Tree of Life. That which Adam had forfeited through sin at the beginning of the world, will be restored in the eternal realm of heaven.

The earlier letter to the Ephesians from Paul, as well as this shorter version from John was written for the ordinary people who walked the streets of Ephesus – the butcher, the baker, the candlestick maker. But imagine if you received this letter today through the post. What would you make of it? Firstly, the man who sent it was not the author – it was a holy letter, sent from the One they believed in, the

One who was the focal point for all their acts of service and was now in heaven. Secondly, in a few short words the Lord accurately pointed to the root cause of their failings as a church – their lack of love for Him, their Saviour.

God knows us intimately and recognises what we do

We all like to be commended for working hard – even if it is not in an obvious way. Every Christmas in the medical practice where I used to work, all the staff received a voucher and card from the doctors. But it was not just a simple card. Every doctor had signed it with a sentence commending our hard work – they used complimentary language, which made us feel good about ourselves. It was affirmation that we were doing the right thing, that somewhere along the line we managed to carry out our work to the best of our ability and someone else had seen and noted that work. Not only is this affirmation but it empowers and motivates greater work, despite the challenges.

Every now and again, Jesus gives us an affirming conversation. It might be in the shape of a friend who takes us out for coffee and says thank you for sitting through a hospital appointment. It might be a work colleague who tells us we are doing well. Or it might be another church member who sends an email to say that was an encouraging word you gave them as they hurried out of the church. To give and receive encouragement is a rich spiritual gift commended by Paul (1 Cor 1:5). John's third letter is a wonderful example of encouragement to a young man named Gaius. He had been hospitable to strangers and was walking in the truth, a simple letter yet full of affirmation for what this young man was doing. Practice this spirit of encouragement, for to do the opposite and offer discouragement only demotivates and paralyses our brothers and sisters in Christ.

God had seen the work that the Ephesians had been doing and he wanted John to write down a compliment to their hard work. In fact, it was not just hard graft, but also perseverance and endurance that they had applied to the work every day. Often the going got tough, yet still they kept on going. They persevered and continued to do the work that the Holy Spirit was giving them to do even when they must have felt like giving up. Paul had seen this when staying with them for three years. They had steadfastly refused to allow sexual immorality into their church even though the city was dedicated to Artemis the goddess of female nature. Legend has it that she had purportedly asked to remain a virgin for all her immortal days, yet the city promoted immoral practices. In the centre of this immoral city the church had remained pure.

Yes, says our Lord – I know you, what you do, your perseverance in the darkness, your commitment to this church that I have placed you in. I know what you do. I am watching, moving amongst you as I did on Earth. The beautiful picture that John supplies us with at the beginning of Revelation is of Jesus walking amongst the lamp stands (1:13) those very churches that he was talking to now. But it is a holy walk, one where reverence and awe follow him like a golden trail. John himself wrote in his first letter that the walk of Jesus is one of love (2: 5,6) and if we want to be like him, as we are commanded to be, it is in obedience that we will find the completeness of love. In Deuteronomy (23: 12–14) there is a picture of the holiness of God put next to the very human nature of man. God told the Israelites that when they wanted to relieve their bowels they were to do so outside the camp and ensure that they dug a hole (even commanding them to have a spade with them when they went) to use as a lavatory and then cover up the results with soil. This was not so much to do with hygiene but was rather so that as God moved about among them he would not have to look on the results of man's sinfulness (the sin that had removed him from the garden of Eden) and so turn away. The excretion of our bodies appears to be an unholy thing in the social commands from God to the Israelites. It is indicative of the 'matter' that we excrete through our mouths because of what we ingest through our eyes and ears. God alone knows exactly what our hearts contain and so he bids us repent.

Main Street of Ephesus

God is so holy that we should be aware of those things that we allow into our churches; neighbourhood; houses and lives. What do you allow in your house that might give you spiritual indigestion – pictures in magazines or on the television or computer that keep returning to your mind when you are supposed to be dwelling on the richness of Christ and the pictures of heaven that he gives? How, asks the Lord of the Ephesian church, are you going to keep your love for me pure and unadulterated? There was still the passion for hard work but the motivation that drove those acts had become blurred by the hard work itself and the person of the Lord Jesus Christ had been lost. This happens so easily today where community work starts out with a heightened feeling of a desire to bring Jesus to people and then over a period, that passion turns into a business and a whole system of employment. The face of the Lord can no longer be seen in what was once his work and secularization creeps in by the back door.

To receive such a letter from a little-known island on which their oldest apostle was incarcerated must have made every member of the Ephesian church sit up and listen hard. They were hearing things about themselves that they had neither admitted or recognised. Reading the voice of their Lord out loud in the centre of the congregation their hearts must have swelled as they heard him say that he knew what they were going through living amid a godless city. He knew that they were hard working and that they were persevering despite the idolatry and wickedness all around them. He commended their insight and wisdom when it came to determining men who preach from scripture and those who entertain for their own sake. This was empowering words from the Saviour Himself. Well done! Keep going!

However, with the next words of the letter their mouths must have dropped open as suddenly they realised with insight and clarity of mind given them by the Holy Spirit that they were not in such a good place as they had arrogantly thought.

Passion slippage!

It is at this point that the letter changes tone. Paul's letter to the Ephesians warned specifically about keeping pure so that the devil would not get a foothold (Ephesians 5:3). He had told them repeatedly, having been amongst them for three years preaching, that they must be careful, warning each family member, employee, and employer about the way they were to interact with each other and amongst unbelievers. But they had apparently let their armour slip despite being reminded so many times that alertness is required of a soldier. Somehow the belt of truth had come undone; the extra weight of indolent living had snapped the buckle. The breast plate had become rusty and the hinges no longer clicked into place. They were wearing slippers instead of running shoes and the shield was hanging on the wall for decoration only. The protective head gear was left behind in the hope of herd immunity from an apparently happy church. Their sword was unsharpened and unused in the attic as a distant memory of battles once fought – a talisman against the undiscussed future. We must be aware of running from the enemy but then exposing our backs – for these protective garments are all to the front. We must face our enemy prepared with the shield and protective garments given by God himself.

Despite the history that the Ephesian Christians had and the reputation that they had amongst the other Asian churches, there was something not quite right. They had been going along with the normal ups and downs of church life, but rather than being proactive in keeping themselves pure and holy, they were instead allowing the world to become a part of the church and were in danger of having no distinguishable features from the world. They had become 'secular Christians.' They were losing their Christ like characteristics and becoming self-focused instead. Rather than being transformed by the renewing of their minds they were in fact conforming to the world (Romans 12: 2). Paul says decisively that to be transformed, we must not conform to the pattern of this world, but rather to the pattern of Christ.

When God gave instructions to Moses for the building of the desert tabernacle he repeatedly said that it must be made 'exactly like the pattern I show you' (Exodus 25: 9, 40). While God was present dwelling in the tabernacle made according to his holy specifications nothing could harm them. But the minute they allowed contamination to come in from outside they lost that protection. We too must stay away from the pattern of this world that harms our inner being, and instead follow the pattern of living as set down by Jesus while on earth (John 17:15-18). That pattern is one of holiness, being set apart from the sinfulness of the world while leaving us right in the centre with the protection and shield of the truth of God.

God gave specific plans to Moses for the priestly garments to be worn by Aaron and his sons when they were going about their duties in the temple (Exodus 28: 1-5). They were sacred garments designed so that they could serve God. The robes were to be made of rich colours – gold, blue, purple, and scarlet, colours that would stand out in a crowd so that onlookers could not fail to recognise who they were. These garments were far beyond the value of what they would normally wear, for they had not earned the richness and royal appearance of these clothes. Yet God wanted them to serve Him dressed in such a way as to glorify his presence and be recognised by the people as His special servants. In the same way God has dressed us, His believing children in robes that are far beyond our worth. We are sinners in His sight, yet because of the sacrificial death of His Son we can put on these clothes and stand in front of a holy God, undeserving yet righteous in His sight. With those clothes on, just like Aaron we become an example to those around us. We should stand out and be recognised for who we are – sinners saved by the grace of God, a new creation, transformed and clothed in garments of wonderful colours and white linen.

What do these clothes look like in our world? Paul describes them to us in Colossians (3:12). These clothes are made of the finest threads: compassion, kindness, humility, gentleness, and patience, but the onus is on us to put them on. While God provides us with the resources, we must do the work of threading the needle and making the garments. For Aaron and his sons, God provided specially gifted people who would make the garments – they had been given the training to make a perfect fit. In the same way, God gathers well trained people around us who will enable us in the making of our own garments, for we cannot learn patience and humility in isolation. We need the direction of others who have trod the path before us to give a helping hand. Similarly, we are required to help those on the path behind us so that no one is struggling alone to pull on ill-fitting or inadequate clothing.

Parkinson (2016) says that those priestly garments that were soiled beyond being retrieved, were shredded, and used to make wicks for the tabernacle lampstand. This is a wonderful picture of how we need to keep a close eye on the spiritual garments that we wear so that we do not get used to their dirtiness. Instead we need to constantly examine them to ensure that they are still white and a witness to the community. We cannot keep linen that we do not need – instead, we need to burn it to completely eradicate any areas of our lives that are not radiating out the love of Christ.

The same caveat that the Lord extended to the Ephesians is also given to us. Satan is there to steal those clothes while they are in the making. He wants to destroy our God given character and make it His, as Jesus warns us (10:10). John is recounting the story of Jesus being the Good Shepherd – the one who really cares for the sheep, not like the thief who wants to steal, kill, and destroy. Because the thief only wants the power from the sale of the sheep he has no feelings for any of them if one breaks away and falls over a cliff. That thief is satan and Jesus tells the Ephesians that they must recognise the tricks that the devil will employ to steal away those beautiful garments that God is dressing them in. We too need to be alert, on guard and ready to dismiss the insidious lies of the devil.

Forsaking their first love in the church at Ephesus and falling from the great heights of their joy in Christ while running after affirmation for their works of service in the world was sinful. Their very first love says Strauch (2008) is for Christ who showed them his love on the cross. But they had lost other loves too. The love for others and for the holy things of God. They had not been alert, or recognised the lies of the devil. Instead, they had fallen and while doing so, the garments that had been in the making had been torn from their backs. The only antidote for the Ephesian church and for us is to see this as sin and repent. Turn around and go back to the reason you became a Christian in the first place. Understand that nothing and no one can save you from the life in this world that you have carved out for yourself, only Jesus Christ who loved you and died for you can save you. Paul said:

'wretched man that I am! Who will rescue me from this body of death? Thanks be to God – through Jesus Christ our Lord!' (Romans 7:24,25).

However, if no repentance is forthcoming, John registers a warning from the mouth of the Lord Jesus as he had been walking amongst the seven golden lamp stands. A lamp stand is a light held up on high to be seen in the darkness, a light in a golden holder. This is no ordinary light in the darkness, but real light encased in royalty – the King of Kings. The light of the world is Jesus Christ, held up high so that He can shed light and be seen. It is this lamp stand – the witness as a church – that will be removed if no repentance is made, for Jesus cannot be a light in the church that is harbouring sin, for that would tarnish His name.

The sin of pride and secularism had crept into the Ephesian church and was insidiously destroying the passion and life that had previously characterised this holy and redeemed church. Jesus was sending them a message to remind them that He was the head of the church and more than that He was their bridegroom. He was walking among the churches then and now. He encourages us and loves us through our sin, wanting us to turn back to Him and not be infected by a sense of self-righteousness or moralistic attitude which then produces pride. Love must be the motivating factor for all we do, because 'love is vital to the survival of our churches today (Strauch, 2008). *We can spend a lifetime building an empire, only for it to be destroyed (Eccl 1:11, 2:11).* Jesus reminds us that the only things that last are those which cannot decay, such as love, faith, hope, kindness, patience, and self-control. There is no place in His church for the insidious nature of secularization which so often characterizes our churches today.

In Acts (20:17-38), Paul gave a very emotional farewell to the Ephesian Elders. He told them that he would never see them again but urged them to remember everything he had taught them and to continue being alert – a recurring theme to the Ephesians, for they were living in a world of idol worship which is no different today. Paul's final message to them was that it is more blessed to give than receive, the central theme of his letter to the Ephesians. In everything we do we should first be the servant to others, to serve them as Jesus has served us, to love them as He has loved us. And now here in John's letter to that same church, he says somewhere along the line the motivation for what they were doing has dwindled, causing their actions to lose their focus.

We cannot escape that all seeing and all-knowing God for He walks this earth watching us continually. Yet it is with a loving hand that He gently pulls us back to the centre of his universe. He knows just how easy it is to drift away, without noticing that anything has changed. On holiday or at weekends, when everything is calm and going along normally, with scarcely a cloud on the horizon, I find it so easy to forget to pray or read my bible, partly because I am out of my routine but also because I have lost my focus on Jesus Christ and am focusing instead on my own desires. So how do we make sure we don't drift on a tide of the world's comings and goings? How do we keep a close eye on how much our lives are integrating with worldly instead of Godly pleasures? Prepare for that holiday time or retirement by rekindling a desire to retain a focus on God Himself. Be prepared with a subject to read around or write in a journal about; meditate and reflect employing minds in a Godly pursuit rather than just letting ourselves wander through novels which do not demand challenges from us. You and I are continuing sinners – not once a sinner and now no longer. Sin is serious and grows if allowed to take root, but it is that recognition which keeps us from pride; keeps us humble and passionate about our witness because we know what we have been given and are being saved from in eternity.

Eternal Blessing and the Glorious Reward

Paul's letter to the Ephesians was a picture of the kind of garments that we are given by God to be dressed appropriately as His bride. It describes the wonderful way in which God redeemed us, what He had to do to pay the redemption cost, the 'clothes' each member of the family is to wear, and how we are to protect ourselves on the journey. Submission for each other is like undergarments: the love in a marriage which should be examples of Christlike love for His church; obedience from children for their parents and respect for employers. But what happens when we forget that armour, forget the clothes we have been given for the journey? We are then unprotected and vulnerable, tempted by the things of the world which we allow to slip into our lives without even noticing. We live in the same culture as Ephesus, where sexual immorality is seen on all the pages of our newspapers. We tolerate things that we should not, according to God's word, and we allow sin into our churches because of our desire to be politically correct which is greater than our desire to serve God. We tolerate bad language; taking the Lord's name in vain; sexual deviation and immorality because the lines of spiritual morality have been blurred in our attempt to be nonjudgmental and diversity is given a higher standing than the commands of God.

Everyone does what is right in their own eyes just as they have been doing for thousands of years (Judges 21:25). But the spiritual code in the Bible is based on love. Love which does not judge; is patient; kind; rejoices in truth and is not self-seeking (1 Cor 13: 4-6) and is always ready to learn from each other. The Ephesian church had moved away from the words of Jesus given to His apostles and were living for themselves and their service rather than for Christ. This meant that they had lost their focus on what was eternal, which was of so much more value and certainty than the future around them.

The results of coming back to the Lord and recommitting to Him are beyond anything that we could possibly imagine. Paul wrote to the Ephesians (3:20) that they would not be able to imagine the glory of the future church if they let the power of Christ work through them. In this letter, Jesus said that God will give the right to eat from the Tree of Life (Rev 22:2), presently in the paradise of God, to all those who overcome this world's temptations. The Tree of Life in Genesis was described as one of two trees, the other one being the Tree of the Knowledge of good and evil. Adam was instructed that he could eat of any other seed-bearing plant but not the Tree of the Knowledge of good and evil. The tree of life maintained their immortality, but when they disobeyed God and instead ate from the tree of knowledge, immortality was denied, and they suffered the punishment of death (Alcorn, 2004).

Adam bore vicarious responsibility for his wife and allowed her to do what God had expressly told them not to do, and in fact colluded with her in her disobedience. The serpent stood beside the tree, having lured the woman through her own temptation, rubbing his hands with glee and shouting in triumph to God that he had won. Knowledge of good and evil allowed man the immediate recognition of his own frail humanity and sinfulness and he was expelled from that close relationship with his creator. Satan was given an eternal punishment and the serpent who harbored the devil was condemned to a life on the ground (Gen 3:14). Returning to that paradise in close communion with God will allow man to eat from the Tree of Life again and so live forever with God.

In this letter to the church in Ephesus Jesus says that those who see what is happening and repent by returning to their first love, will be able to eat from the Tree of Life in paradise where it is presently until the new heaven and new earth (Rev

22: 2) are populated. This is not a removal of those people who were truly saved from the Kingdom of God. Rather this is a warning to those Christians who choose to live a life that does not focus on the Lord Jesus. They will forfeit the joy and peace so characteristic of believers and will have their lampstand of witness removed so that they cannot damage the Kingdom of God.

This is our hope – an expectation of everlasting life referred to as our reward and the hope which we continually look towards, not because we have earned it, but because we have been given it through grace alone. This is the glorious truth in which we can boast, because it comes not through our doing but as a gift for every believer in the Lord Jesus Christ. As believers, we look beyond death, which comes as a release from our sinfulness, towards this blessed and glorious hope of eternity with Christ.

Jesus wants to give us the blessing that He has prepared for us. Imagine if you had worked for years on a special gift to give the one you loved and then when it came time to give it, that person turned away and said they did not want it because they preferred other things? That is what happens when we dismiss God who has given us the precious gift of His Son Jesus and the promise of eternal life.

This letter finishes in a similar way to some of the others. God has given us the ability to hear what He is saying, so listen carefully. This message came from the mouth of the Lord Jesus Christ especially for you and me – we must listen to benefit from the reward that He has died to give us. For in hearing, really hearing, you will be able to enjoy all that eternal life has to offer you, which is God's gift, as well as being able to eat from the Tree of Life.

In writing down these messages from his Lord as He walked amongst the lamp stands, John must have realised afresh how much God cared for and loved His Church. He praises us for our deeds of strength during trials and our perseverance when life is hard. He wants us to survive – and to survive with joy in our hearts that comes from true repentance, reaching the potential that He places within each church using all the gifts that are showered upon us in order that we might glorify His Father.

Then we can share with the Lord Jesus Christ an eternity in the paradise of God.

'I am not ashamed of the gospel, because it is the power of God for the salvation of everyone who believes: first for the Jew and then for the Gentile.' Romans 1:16

Reflection:

1. At the beginning of the letter Jesus held in his right hand the seven stars. These were the angels or messengers to the seven churches. Today we are given a similar task, as the perfect number of messengers who are given good news to be stars shining in a dark world. We only see stars at night when it is dark. During the day they do not go into hiding, we just cannot see them. At night, their beauty is to be seen and we marvel at their display in the darkness. What did Jesus do to show that He was the light of the world? How do you shine in the darkness of our world, a beautiful light in the darkness?

2. What kind of wild beasts did Paul fight in Ephesus (1 Cor 15:32)? Were they literal, or were they beasts of the mind and spirit? What are your wild beasts? What motivates you daily to ensure that you are alert to Satan's insidious temptations to conform to the pattern of this world?

3. The following is an extract from Christianity Today 2004:

The state of the contemporary church in Turkey, home to so many seminal moments in Christian history, looks bleak for now. Perhaps integration into the European Union will galvanize the small Greek Orthodox community in Istanbul and allow the Turkish government to honestly examine the grizzly fate of the Armenians. Hopefully, the spread of religious freedom there will ease hostility toward missionaries and converts from Islam to Christianity. Regardless, we should heed the warnings of history—beware the dangers of political infighting between Christians with earthly interests at heart, and never underestimate the seriousness of Islamic jihad.

What kind of hostility to Christianity exists in the Western World? How do you deal with the thought of persecution both here and in the East?

In light of the above what do you think is the future of churches that do not heed the warning of the letter to the church at Ephesus – 'If you do not repent, I will come to you and remove your lampstand from its place?'

Jesus asked the Ephesians to return to their first love and we are called to encourage one another with the reason for our faith remembering that our Lord is coming again soon. Listen to this song on https://www.youtube.com/watch?v=Ht5QvAMDMzE and be reminded that the King of glory will soon come on the clouds of glory. The author Brooke Fraser is a New Zealand singer song writer with Hillsong Worship.

The Letter to the Church at Smyrna

Summary to the Church at Smyrna

Known as the 'Port of Asia', Smyrna was the home of the martyred Polycarp. A place where both the Jews and the Romans persecuted the Christians, so much so that they lived in extreme poverty, running the gauntlet of continual torture and martyrdom for the sake of Christ.

However, this was the only church that the Lord praised without any caveats. They were on their knees both physically through suffering and in their prayers. The Lord gave them encouragement from heaven, to continue and keep looking up beyond their present sufferings.

Suffering comes to everyone who lives here on earth – it is part of the heritage of man and we cannot escape it. But God gives us the picture of His Son who suffered for our sake and asks us to look beyond our challenges and hardships towards the day when the crown of life becomes ours forever.

Now read on...................

John's memories of the Church at Smyrna

The second letter was to be sent to Smyrna. As John listened to the words, he heard Jesus saying to these tortured and martyred Christians not to be afraid. He thought of the many times he had met Christians from the church in Smyrna, sometimes secretly so that they would not be punished for his presence, encouraging them not to be afraid of what man can do – for nothing can separate us from the love of God that is in Christ Jesus our Lord.

To the church in Smyrna:

Revelation 2: 8-11 (NLT)

'Write this letter to the angel of the church in Smyrna.

This is the message from the one who is the First and the Last, who was dead but is now alive:

I know about your suffering and your poverty—but you are rich! I know the blasphemy of those opposing you. They say they are Jews, but they are not, because their synagogue belongs to Satan. Don't be afraid of what you are about to suffer. The devil will throw some of you into prison to test you. You will suffer for ten days. But if you remain faithful even when facing death, I will give you the crown of life.

Anyone with ears to hear must listen to the Spirit and understand what he is saying to the churches. Whoever is victorious will not be harmed by the second death.'

With love from the Father through his servant,

John

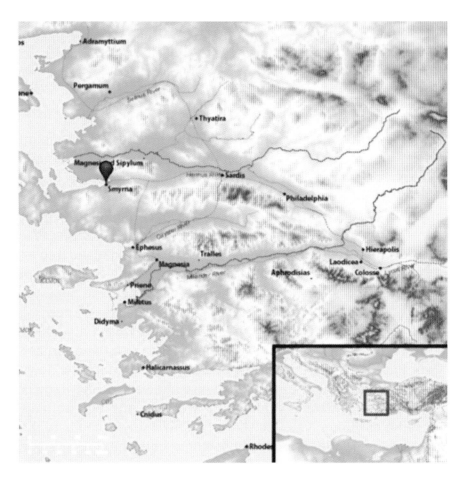

Biblios Maps

History of Smyrna and the Church

Smyrna is present day Izmir in Turkey and 25 miles north of Ephesus. A patriotic city, Smyrna had the greatest temple built outside Rome to the goddess Britannia. This goddess belonged to a small group of islands on the edge of the known world, the main island of which was Britannia, now the United Kingdom. Smyrna was also called the 'Port of Asia' because of its Aegean harbour. It was and is a beautiful city. Its destruction by war some few hundred years before Jesus was born caused it to be rebuilt magnificently by able architects. Boasting a significant stadium and library, it is the birthplace of Homer and adulates the Roman Emperor, raising him to god like status. Witnessing for Christ in a place like Smyrna where hero worship was the cultural norm was never going to be easy. The Christians refused to worship Caesar, although they would pray for him. The Jews hated the Christians because they were allowed the privilege of not worshipping Caesar and did not want anyone else to have that same privilege. The Christians in Smyrna were poor to the point of abject poverty, possibly because both the Romans and the Jews had extorted them to the point of penury. Not only were they poor but they suffered from extreme slander. People were going around saying that they were cannibals as they ate the Lord's body and drank the blood of Jesus Christ when they took the bread and the wine.

Smyrna itself was rich in mined materials one of which was antimony – a metal compound used for flame proofing materials, as well as black eye make up for the Egyptian queens. It was discovered in 1600 BC and was a rich reminder of the flame proofing that was given to these faithful Christians by God himself. They were ultimately protected from the flames of the devil, persecution and suffering by their faith in the Lord Jesus Christ because their reward was in knowing they would be kept safe for eternity. Though their persecution often led to death they were not afraid of the flames of martyrdom.

It was probable that John met the Bishop of Smyrna, Polycarp, who lived from 69-155 AD (Nickens 2005). There is no statement in the Bible as to John's physical presence in the city but as it was only a few miles distant from Ephesus and John was one of the few surviving people who had seen the Lord, it would seem improbable not to have met. Polycarp became a believer in Christ when quite young and made bishop of the church in Smyrna where later he was burnt as a martyr at the age of 86, determined to make a stand for his Lord. The letter to Smyrna commended its martyrs knowing that the Christians there suffered much persecution and torture. Polycarp was known to be an encourager of the other churches writing to the church in Philippi quoting 1 John 4:3 *'every spirit that does not acknowledge Jesus is not from God. This is the spirit of the antichrist, which you have heard is coming and even now is already in the world.'* Another young protégé of Polycarp, Irenaeus wrote that he knew Polycarp had 'had conversations with John and with the rest of those who had seen the Lord.' A year after Polycarp's death it was recorded (Christianity Today 2018) that the smell of his martyrdom was 'not as burning flesh but as bread baking or as gold and silver refined in a furnace.' The Christians in Smyrna had learnt their lessons of faithfulness from those who went before proclaiming the name of Jesus Christ.

Smyrna today is a flourishing city with many Christian churches working for God in a spiritual hungry land in contrast to the ruined cities of Ephesus and Sardis, both now only villages. After visiting Izmir, Stetzer (2011) described it as 'spiritually charged', a hard-pressed city still persecuted in the heart of Turkey.

Today, Jesus walks amongst the lampstands of the world and the city of Izmir's lampstand shines brightly for all to see.

The mark of the Christians from a pavement in Ephesus

Message to the Church at Smyrna and application

Lily Gaynor asked her friend Helen what her biggest challenge was as a missionary (Gaynor and Butterworth 2013). She thought the answer would be finance. She had come to the point in the middle of her African mission where she was burnt out with no money or resources and wondered how she could keep going. No, her friend answered, it is not about money, but rather 'to keep the fire burning in my own heart.'

Finance Lily discovered, was God's problem not hers. She came to realise her responsibility was to keep the fire burning in her own heart and God gave her three messages:

1. In Leviticus (6: 8–14) three times God repeats the phrase 'keep the fire burning.' The ashes must be cleared out every morning otherwise the fire will become clogged up, even with tiny ash particles. These are unrecognized sins of thought and word that need daily confession and clearing away. If they are left, the heart becomes blocked with unconfessed sin and the passion or fire of faith will die out.

2. The fire needs daily fuel, recognising that not all wood is good fuel. Some will just make the fire smoke, and others will put a fire out. It may look acceptable but if it is putting out the fire of God then don't use it. Discern what you take into your spiritual life – reading; watching; time consuming hobbies or projects and know that the best fuel is God's word.

3. It is a daily sacrifice because the purpose of the fire is to consume the offering. We need a daily dying to self (Rom 12: 1, 2); to our rights; our pride; our comforts and all that goes to make up our own ego. It is a daily taking up of the cross not just to carry it but to die on it, so that we ourselves diminish and Christ our Lord increases, in all His glory.

This was the message to the church at Smyrna and for us today, keep the fire of passion for Christ burning so that you can withstand all the challenges that come your way. Jesus reminded them that He was in control of the whole world and therefore of the persecution they were going through. Suffering for the Lord is transitory, for a limited period, after which comes the reward.

The Persecuted Church

This letter reaffirms the validity and absolute truth of the death and resurrection of Jesus Christ. But it is so easy for us to forget this fundamental truth of the gospel of Jesus Christ. He gave us a way of remembering him on a regular basis, as previously mentioned. It is in the regular taking of the bread and wine, the feast instituted by our Lord Jesus Christ on the night of the Passover (Luke 22:19), that we remind ourselves of the death that ended all deaths. Although John himself did not record this remembrance feast, he gave us the underpinning evidence for the sacrificial love of Jesus (John 17: 23, 24). As believers come together in their love for the One who died to save them, so they will be united in the message they take across the world (John 17:20–23). If we forget to remind ourselves of this fact, it will become a story, a vague historic happening rather than a certainty and a daily part of our living. If we only attend church to take communion then we are missing the point that John makes – to love one another in the highs and the lows of each other's lives through that continuing fellowship of meeting regularly. If our sin is so severe that it paralyses us, then we have also forgotten that Jesus is making us clean through an ongoing process (John 15:3). We cannot exist in isolation, Jesus said, we need the main vine, which is Himself, to survive (John 15:1,2). Sometimes God takes us to a place where we need to examine ourselves in the light of Christ, asking whether we are doing as He commanded to be a light to the community. If you feel you are in that place, then place yourself before the Lord to ask His forgiveness and to reinstate you in the place where He wants you to be His light.

God remains in control of His church and of the entire world that He has created (Psalm 2). Nothing happens in this world without the knowledge of God (Acts 17: 24–31). He understands the beginning from the end because He has seen it before it happened and knows how the story of earth is going to finish. We are now at the point in history where the start of that ending is about to happen. No-one knows the day or time when Jesus will return – only the Father, but it will be as surprising as a thief coming in the night (1 Thessalonians 5: 2). So, He calls us to expect Him at any time and to be ready in whatever situation we find ourselves. Yet why in the meantime does the church have to suffer? For if Christ loves His church surely he can rescue it from persecution. Jesus told us to expect to suffer for His sake and John penned these words of Jesus from the night of His betrayal:

'If the world hates you, keep in mind that it hated me first. If you belonged to the world, it would love you as its own. As it is, you do not belong to the world, but I have chosen you out of the world. That is why the world hates you.' John 15: 18,19

So, this is not a mystery – Jesus had prophesied it and with good reason. The Jewish leaders of His day were jealous for their own place in society – they had been the teachers of the law and now someone was threatening their position. But more than that, their whole way of life and culture was being thrown up into the air like a pack of cards. Jesus had turned them on their heads and told them to love their enemies and this they could not do. They had no love in their hearts to offer Romans or the Gentiles and they did not want to accept the love that Jesus offered them to enable them to love others.

There are many parts of the world today where Christians are being persecuted. Jamil, a former Yemeni Muslim, but now a follower of Jesus Christ, shares a unique insight into the body of Christ in Yemen (Open Doors 2019) where, at the time of writing, there has been a vicious civil war going on for two years.

"As Christians we feel like strangers in our own country. The war has focused us on what really matters—following Christ— even if it costs us our lives. The Bible is very clear about what we can expect; suffering is part of life for those who follow Christ. Therefore many Yemeni Christians long for Jesus to return. We lost so much; we reach out to the everlasting peace that He will bring one day—hopefully soon!"

Jamil was born and raised in Yemen to a Muslim family. As a young man he got to know Christ and started following Him. This cost him most of his relationships within his family. *"Yemeni Muslims are raised with the idea that converting to Christianity should lead to immediate exclusion from your family and tribe, and of course you'll have to suffer the wrath of Allah."*

Jamil migrated out of Yemen before the war started, but he regularly returns to encourage his Christian brothers and sisters. A lot has changed for Yemeni Christians since the war started, Jamil notices. *"The violence has affected the church enormously. Many Christians had to leave their communities; they are now scattered all over the country,"* Jamil shares. *"It may sound strange, but the fact that many Christian families had to flee has become a huge blessing. There are Christians everywhere in the country now, not just in certain pockets. And the faith is growing because, as Christians, we seem to have lost our fear. Through the crisis and the war God has empowered us to share the Gospel wherever we are."*

Jamil I am sure would have resonated with the believers in Smyrna – his desire for the return of the Lord Jesus far outweighs the fear of torture and persecution – in fact they expect it from the moment they turn their backs on Islam and take the pathway that leads them to Christ. To these persecuted Christians and sometimes martyrs, this fact makes them rich beyond the confines of this world and gives them a peace past understanding. God's word teaches that we must love one another, leave all jealousy, covetousness, grumblings, and sexual immorality behind us, and step out into God's way of living. It means repenting of our lifestyle and admitting that we were wrong, and God was right. The many who will not do this, hate the ones who have chosen God in their lives.

Polycarp left a legacy of his attitude to the persecutors of Smyrna's day. The proconsul of Smyrna asked him to recant, but his reply has lived as an encouragement to all persecuted Christians since then:

'Eighty and six years have I served Christ and he never did me any injury, how then can I blaspheme my King and Saviour? Thou threatenest me with fire which burns for an hour and after a little while is extinguished, but art ignorant of the fire of the coming judgment and the eternal punishment reserved for the ungodly'.

Transitory suffering

God rarely gives us answers in the way that we would imagine, but instead helps us look past the suffering to something meaningful and beautiful that He has created for us. Smyrna means myrrh, used in death to preserve, and stop the smell of decay. Mary the mother of Jesus had been given the gift of myrrh when He was born, after which He lived His life in the light of the sacrifice He was going to make for the world. Jesus will stop the smell of death and decay in our lives as we give a sacrifice of ourselves to Him just as Smyrna did in its day. Jesus told this church to rejoice in the knowledge that He identified with them in their suffering. He knew about each individual persecution they were going through as He too had suffered as they were suffering. Smyrna was a beautiful church, so poor in terms of the world but richer than the richest man on Earth. They gave despite their suffering because they loved just as their Lord Jesus had loved. It was their suffering that had made them beautiful, not in their own eyes but in the eye of the all-seeing God.

Why is it we are so afraid of suffering? In suffering we are not in control of our own destiny, for we are in pain and made vulnerable. Bereavement or the unexpected finish of a close relationship cruelly cuts up the expectations we have for our lives. Jesus says tells us not to be afraid, especially in death (1 Corinthians 15: 54). And why were they not to be afraid? Because He has overcome all things, and this is not all there is for more is coming that we cannot imagine:

'No eye has seen, no ear has heard, no mind has conceived what God has prepared for those who love him.' 1 Corinthians 2:9

All people will die a first death, but believers in Christ will only experience that first physical death, apart from those who are here at the second coming of Christ. Those who are still here when Christ comes will be taken up to meet Him in the air (1 Thessalonians 4:17). Those who do not believe in the living God and in His Son will experience the second death which is eternal separation from God described in graphic detail at the end of Revelation (Revelation 20: 14,15). None of the believers in Smyrna were going to suffer a second death because they were all saved by the power and grace of a loving God. God remains just and cannot renege on His ageless covenant with man – the promises of God will never be broken (Gen 2: 17). Many find this a difficult concept because they think heaven is either a natural progression, their rite of passage, or have no belief in an afterlife – even some Jews do not believe in the resurrection of the dead. God will never break His promise and as a holy righteous God, He must judge those who are not righteous; we can only be saved from this second death by the blood of the Lord Jesus Christ, there is no other way to be saved from an eternal hell (Acts 4: 12). It is blood that atones for our sin (Leviticus 17:11), which was the reason for Christ's death on the cross for sinful man.

This bigger picture was the reason for transitory suffering, in other words a momentary and fleeting passing of time, compared to the years of eternity in heaven. The people from Smyrna were to suffer for ten days, a short period of time only, for suffering does not last. Philippians (4:4–6) tells us to rejoice in everything, to give thanks all the time even for the suffering that we are passing through. Not necessarily for the root cause of the suffering which may be because of man's evil intent. But give thanks for the way in which God is guiding us through that suffering and for the hint of blessing that we feel as we pass through. After which we can experience the heavenly peace that reigns in the heart of the believer who finds rest with the eternal God.

Judgement from a righteous and holy God is a reality that nobody can run away from, despite many attempts to do so. It is right to be afraid of death when the body dies with a soul that has not been saved from the second death. But to die knowing that we are going to live eternally with God removes all fear from that process. How can we know that we are saved? By accepting Jesus Christ, the Son of God into our hearts as the Christians did in those early days of Smyrna. In the place of fear we can experience the fearlessness of a deathless life and tell others of this marvelous message of peace.

As Christians today, we are encouraged to remain faithful, knowing that the promises of God will never be broken. Through even the fiercest of storms we can depend on a God who loves us beyond our understanding.

'In all these things we are more than conquerors through him who loved us. For I am convinced that neither death nor life, neither angels nor demons, neither the present nor the future, nor any powers, neither height nor depth, nor anything else in all creation, will be able to separate us from the love of God that is in Christ Jesus our Lord.' Romans 8: 37–39

The love of God in Christ Jesus extends beyond the known world. There are powers and dominions that we have never experienced known only to God. There is a power trying to break that love which God will never allow to be broken. God will judge the living and the dead and those who are His own, who believe in His Son Jesus Christ, will be given the crown of life. It is in the faithfulness of believing, regardless of life's circumstances, that the Lord promises the crown of life to the Smyrnians. James (1: 12) says that the man who perseveres under trials of many kinds, will receive this crown, because God has promised it to those who love Him. The promise of eternal life is a royal gifting, denoting honour and blessing as heirs in the Kingdom of God. When the crown is put on the head of a new King or Queen, it says that this person has been given power and authority to rule until the end of their lives. The crown of eternal life will be given by the one whose power is omnipotent and everlasting. It is there waiting for us to receive when our Life's work on earth is finished.

Reflection

1. What is your greatest challenge as a Christian, living in a world that is not Christ centred?

2. What do you think are the riches that you have in Christ which are worth far more than any of your worldly goods, necessary though they might be to daily living?

3. How are you dealing with the 'transitory suffering' that you are experiencing in your life?

Regardless of the tumult around us the Lord asks us to be thankful for His mercy and love which surrounds us. Robert Lowry originally published this song in the 1869 song book, Bright Jewels for the Sunday School, writing the music to words which were possibly written by the original Quakers although never used publicly. Many musicians have added and subtracted verses, but the same message has remained over the centuries, that no storm can shake my inmost calm, while to the rock I am clinging. https://www.youtube.com/watch?v=hazlblps5DQ

The Letter to the Church at Pergamum

Summary of the letter to the Church at Pergamum

Pergamum was the world's centre for medicine during the Roman times. Intellectualism was the god of the students and academics. An immense temple shadowed the city with an altar dedicated to Satan.

The church had fallen prey to false teaching listening to the academics who thought they knew more than God, causing the Christians to become guilty of intellectual idol worship. Despite living under the shadow of satan worship the Lord praised their commitment to his name and their resilience under such spiritual pressure.

Today the church needs to be on guard and recognise the idols that come in by the back door claiming attention and removing our focus from God.

Now read on......................

John's memories of the Church at Pergamum

The next city on the west of Turkey was Pergamum, built on top of a hill one thousand feet above sea level. John could see the city in his mind's eye – he had been there often, climbed the hill into the natural fortress, prayed with the Christians there regarding the idol worship that was so prevalent. Now a message from God himself was to penetrate straight into the satanic atmosphere that pervaded Pergamum.

The Letter to the Church at Pergamum

Revelation 2: 12-17 NLT

'Write this letter to the angel of the church in Pergamum.'

Dear Brothers and Sisters at Pergamum,

'This is the message from the one with the sharp two-edged sword:

I know that you live in the city where Satan has his throne, yet you have remained loyal to me. You refused to deny me even when Antipas, my faithful witness, was martyred among you there in Satan's city.

But I have a few complaints against you. You tolerate some among you whose teaching is like that of Balaam, who showed Balak how to trip up the people of Israel. He taught them to sin by eating food offered to idols and by committing sexual sin. In a similar way, you have some Nicolaitans among you who follow the same teaching. Repent of your sin, or I will come to you suddenly and fight against them with the sword of my mouth.

Anyone with ears to hear must listen to the Spirit and understand what he is saying to the churches. To everyone who is victorious I will give some of the manna that has been hidden away in heaven. And I will give to each one a white stone, and on the stone will be engraved a new name that no one understands except the one who receives it.'

With the blessedness that comes through knowing Christ Jesus,

The Apostle John

Biblios Maps

History of the city and the Church at Pergamum

Pergamum (meaning marriage) was 25 miles inland from the west coast of Turkey, now the modern city of Bergama. It overlooks a large river, Caicus, (known today as Bakircay) and was the seat of emperor worship, home to one of the seven wonders of the world – the Temple of Zeus. The healing god Asclepius came in the form of a serpent (the twisted symbol of healing medicine today) and the city boasted a medical university with a library of over two hundred thousand volumes. The reason for this enormous library resource was because the Egyptians did not like the thought of a rival library to theirs in Alexandria so prohibited the export of papyri to Asia. Pergamum started to make its own parchment out of treated sheep and calf skins which was more durable than papyri and was also exportable and so its library expanded. The name Pergamum is still alive today, in Spanish and Italian as pergamino, meaning parchment. It was a city of intellectualism which had become as much of a god as the stone image of Zeus himself. It had lost the status previously enjoyed as the most important city in Asia, to the nearby city of Ephesus in 133 BC (Violatti 2015). Over the next three hundred years, the city's metropolis foundered as Christianity made a real impact on the worship of the gods and the great temples fell into disrepair. Pergamum as a city, however, was reduced to archeological remains during the seventh century and the Christian church all but disappeared from the map.

The huge altar which sat atop the hill, now housed in a museum in Berlin, is possibly Satan's throne in John's letter to the church (Yeomans 2018). Named as the Great Altar, it attracted visitors from across the Mediterranean, so great was its satanic pull. Pergamum's hospital, known as an Asklepion, after the god, was a centre for healing across the Western Mediterranean and boasted many spas and meditation centers. Affected replica body parts were offered as sacrifices to heal another patient usually as votives (ceramic pieces). For instance, Fabia Secunda presented a gilded bronze ear to the hospital in ancient Pergamum because her ear was healed in a dream. Galen, one of the world's foremost physicians was born here in 126 AD, performing many operations still used today such as the removal of cataracts. There was no better place to study medicine than Pergamum and it was here that all the intellects of the known world gathered.

Today for the first time in a century the Turkish government has authorised the building of a new Christian church in Bergama, the Syriac Orthodox Church (Mintz 2015). Will the lampstand of the church in Pergamum be resurrected as the Lord walks among them?

Archeological remains of the Temple of Diana in Western Turkey

Message for the Church at Pergamum and application

This letter to Pergamum points out three areas that we need to consider in our churches today:

1. The Word of God, which is sharp and double edged, is the only authority by which we as believers in His name should copy as an example for living in this world.

2. Repentance remains a key standard by which we as Christians must live out our time as we struggle against the tide that continually threatens to push us out of existence. Above all we are required to repent of the idol of intellectualism which can paralyse our worship of Christ.

3. The name of the Lord Jesus Christ gives us the courage to continue regardless of the world around us. Our name is important to Him for He knows us and calls us by the name that He knows best having given us a new name for heaven.

Sharper than a double-edged sword

Right here in the very centre of satanic worship, where the Great Altar of the Mediterranean stood on a high mountain representing satan's apparent kingship of the known world, Jesus affirms this beleaguered church. It is a little like going to a function knowing nobody, when suddenly someone comes up to you, claps you on the back, and says 'I know you!' What a wonderful feeling to be known, to be noticed and to feel part of the bigger picture.

That is how it is with our Lord – He knows us and walks with us wherever we have occasion to be. He brings other people into our orbit to encourage and support us. Pergamum must have had many visiting Christians as they came into the city to use its libraries and hospitals in the same way that isolated though we might be, other believers are brought to our door to love and care for us. 'I know where you live,' said Jesus, 'I understand the situation you are in and I applaud you for you have had the courage to witness to my name despite the cost.'

Courage to witness in a world that rejects God requires faith, especially in areas where satan is so active. The art of being brave is brought about not by strength or power, but in recognising the fear and still pressing on. The church at Pergamum is praised for their courage and bravery even when persecution was at its greatest and one of their members Antipas was killed for his faith. He remains an unknown martyr to the world, but to our Lord, he is loved and not only named but given an honoured title – my faithful witness. Savour the beauty of those words for they will also be our reward as we witness in difficult situations: the staff room, the neighbourhood, the estate around your church where vandalism is rife, and gangs infiltrate the community. God knows where each one of us endeavors to speak His name and continues to hold us in the palm of His hand, all the while pointing us towards the greatest goal which is eternity with Himself.

Recognition of the power of the word of God should give us the strength to speak out, yet we often overlook it in the busyness of life. So often the word that is sharper than a two–edged sword becomes blunted in our minds and we forget how to wield it when in action. Hebrews (4: 12) describes what that sword looks like and says that the Word of God is so much sharper than anything made by humans. As a fisherman wields his sharp knife and fillets the fish away from skin and bone with remarkable skill we marvel that he doesn't cut himself in the process. The Word of God is two edged and so much more efficient. Not only can it cut through the lies that come from satan via his followers on earth who have been duped by promises of futile power, but it cuts right through our own self–righteousness. For this 'sword' penetrates the heart of every human being – nothing is hidden from it and as the fisherman's fish lies exposed to the world naked and boneless, so we are exposed to the all searching eye of Almighty God.

As we read the Word of God, it will expose our own lies about ourselves, the judgements we make, the smouldering resentment that is waiting to burst into flames, silent anger that cascades out of our mouths unbidden yet straining to be unleashed from sinful hearts. This word is the truth, the only truth that exists within our world. Nothing else comes near it and we cannot be complacent thinking that God will let us off the hook if we are ignorant of what the Bible says. His truth will not be compromised as Lotz (1997) says: *'It is the truth! And you cannot accommodate truth to the world around you or it ceases to be truth!'* In fact, we live in an age when the Bible has never been more available or understandable. We have no excuse, managing to spend great swathes of time on the internet, yet hardly a minute with the unchanging, every present word of the living God.

This sword reminds us of the judgement that God was going to use against those who were practicing teachings not of His Word (Revelation 19:11). For whenever the word of God is read people are cut to the heart seeing themselves as they really are, as in a mirror. But James (1: 25) says that if we really study the word of God and act on it we will be blessed in what we do.

Even though satan may look as though he is triumphing, God will have the last word, nothing will escape His control of our spinning planet. We, just like the Christians in Pergamum, can be faithful Christians living in the centre of satanic worship. For the bride of Christ is dressed in righteousness not her own and it will shine out even in the darkest night. It is this righteousness that gives us resilience to keep going, even although it looks as though satan has the upper hand. It is not in our strength that we witness for the Lord – we go in His strength as Paul said to the Philippians 'I can do everything through him who gives me strength' (4:13). He gives that strength, but we must reach out and take it to have the courage to go forward. Lotz (1997) says that we need to learn discernment: 'How can I discern what is truth in this world? When I learn to hear the master's voice as the loudest voice in my heart.' Beyond the calling of the voices from this world telling of much learning and gaining of power and money through greater knowledge, we need to learn to discern the still small voice of God, who speaks through the wind and the storm the truth of His Word so that we might 'hold firmly to the faith we profess' (Hebrews 4:14). One of the loudest voices in Pergamum was the voice of intellectualism.

Repent of the idol of intellectualism

The church in Pergamum had fallen prey to the intellectualism within their city, compromising Godly standards by justifying unscriptural living. In so doing they were leading members of the church astray, away from the word of God which was so sharp that it could pierce the deepest lies and most complicated motives, exposing them for what they really were. As with all idols that we find in our world, there is often nothing wrong with the philosophy or concept itself. It is the way we as humans corrupt that concept and raise it above God compromising our first love for Christ. We may find ourselves listening to a moral presentation, all true but missing the core message of the gospel of Christ. Social and secular Christianity dangerously presents itself in such a way that everything about such teaching appears to fit within cultural boundaries. However, Pastors and leadership of churches should be aware of the dangers that biblical evasiveness presents to the flocks that they pastor.

We live in constant danger of compromising our faith and witness within the community. We can so easily let the standards of God's Word slip in a desire to be equally fair and loving to all men and women. By so doing, the message of salvation becomes diluted and immoral practices creep into the churches that are specifically forbidden in scripture. In Matthew (6: 24) Jesus said that it is impossible to serve both God and the world, or satan. God himself will come and fight against those who are sitting on the fence or who are actively preaching a message against the Holiness of His Word.

The teaching of Balaam (Numbers 22–24) was a similar story to that of Pergamum. He was well known for his effective curses and blessings and so was brought in as the ideal person, apparently, to deal with the God of the Israelites. He acknowledged the power of Yahweh, but only as another great god – he did not have any true belief in anything unless he was profiting from it. Despite his recognition of a growing understanding in the awesome power of the one true God, his greed for money and power overtook him. Eventually his greed destroyed him, and he was exposed for the corrupt sorcerer that he was. But not before he had enticed the Israelites to commit sin after sin, dragging them down to his low level. We need to ask God to give insight and discernment to our elders and pastors when any new teachings arise that are not to be found in the Word of God. It is of eternal importance that we keep alert so that no one is enticed away from the central doctrine of our salvation in Christ and the pattern that we are given to live, by which we witness of Him who died for us. Pray for your elders and leaders that they will continually seek God's guidance for wisdom to steer the church in the truth of His Word.

The Nicolaitans were a group of believers who stated that to be Christians in the community it was necessary to be a part of the community around them. The problem was that it did not stop at witnessing for Christ as they continued into practices specifically forbidden by God's Word, such as immoral gain, sexual immorality and idol worship. In so doing they also intellectually justified what they were doing, so much so, that many who were perhaps vulnerable in their faith, were enticed away to follow them. These were in fact, all excuses to sin and God does not compromise His judgement on people who lure others away from the faith. Jesus said that those who cause others to sin would be better off with a millstone tied around the neck and thrown into the sea (Luke 17: 2).

Together with Pergamum we are warned against compromise by allowing sin into the church – particularly idolatry and sexual immorality. It is the sword of God that will find people out. God does not dilute His word to gain more members in His kingdom. To flirt with something that is not of His Word, would require God to be less than God and that can never be. God alone is pure, and nothing can come near Him which is tainted with sin – it was for this reason that His Son died so that by grace alone, man can enter the presence of God. We must teach ourselves to hear the voice of God in our hearts, to practice regular reading of the Word of God so that we are ready to discern any compromised teaching either in ourselves or in the church.

Ungodly intellectualism is one of the hardest sins to deal with in the church, because it is often the leaders that are the intellectuals. Leadership is a responsibility given by God in order that His people might be led in the ways of righteousness. The church in Pergamum knew the serpent in their midst – they understood only too well the throne occupied by satan. This letter from the Lord came not a moment too late – it was time to repent of their sinful practices and return to their first love.

We are called to love all people but not their sinful practices; to be humble and not hypercritical or judgmental of others; recognising always our own sinful practices from which we must repent. We must learn to be Christ's example even when it is we who are discriminated against or when it requires courage to stand against the popular tide of the world. Yet at the same time pray for the grace to practice the characteristics of Christ always hoping and persevering with those who do not yet know Him.

A New Name

Jesus commended every one of those who stood true to His name against popular opinion. No matter the cruelty inflicted on those who loved Him, Jesus stood beside them as they courageously uttered his name in the hardest of places. Children brutally sacrificed; women gang raped; men beheaded and all because they were believers in the Lord Jesus Christ and His Father God in a world that seeks only to do what is right in their own eyes. Because of their courage and bravery they will be given some of the hidden manna and a new name. Manna was the main food of the Israelite family for the forty years that they were in the desert between slavery in Egypt and the giving of the promised land. It tasted of coriander seeds, wafers and honey and they gathered it each morning, just enough for each person living in the tents. If they gathered too much it would become mouldy and full of maggots (Exodus 16:14–33).

God was teaching them His concept of need and greed – enough for their daily needs, and no more because he would provide their exact requirements. The Lord commanded Moses to ensure that two litres of manna was put into a golden jar and then placed within the holy ark of the covenant, underneath the lid of atonement (Hebrews 9:4). This manna remained hidden from sight, reminding all subsequent generations of the generosity and love of God for a willful group of people that often disobeyed Him despite His continual watchful eye over them.

What we require in life, said Jesus to the devil in the desert, is to live by the nourishment of both physical bread and every word that comes out of the mouth of God (Matthew 4:4).

Manna represented the physical needs of the Israelites in the desert, hidden in the place where atonement was offered for their sins. We cannot live without the saving blood shed by the Lord Jesus on the cross at Calvary. This is what nourishes us, making us grow even during severe challenges and hardship. Jesus offered the church at Pergamum hidden manna – the true words of the Holy Spirit that would come to them in the fire of persecution, nourishing and guiding them, giving wisdom when they needed it. This manna would be delicious, sweet as honey and yet as nourishing as milk. It was an additional promise of eternal life to the struggling church in Pergamum. They would remember the words of Jesus through John's gospel (John 6:49,50) telling them that the physical manna which sustained their ancestors through the desert was no longer needed. Instead, in the act of offering His own body for the life of the world, Jesus would become the living bread.

To believe this truly with your whole heart recognising that you are the reason Jesus had to die, means that you will live forever with Him. In that act of dying for your sins, as Jesus broke His body on the cross, God ripped the temple curtain in half. No longer did the manna need to be hid from sight, in fact it was no longer needed at all. Instead, evidence of the living bread walked from the tomb on that third day. Belief in what the Lord Jesus Christ did for us means permanent spiritual nourishment as we come to Him daily to provide all our needs.

Along with the hidden manna would be given a white stone – white because it was pure. The Grecians were given a white stone during their games to the winner of each race. On the stone was written their name alone which only the receiver knew. It was the prize for completing the race recognizing the long commitment to training, forsaking all else to win the race. A similar kind of stone was given by judges in court who on pronouncing their verdict would either drop a black or a white stone into a jar depending on judgement or acquittal. Both descriptions fit the white stone given to those who had overcome all temptations and hardships to win that prize which was set before them and gain the crown of righteousness (2 Timothy 4:8). On the day of judgment it is those who have believed who will be given the stone of acquittal, through the grace and mercy of our Lord Jesus Christ. We are warned of the serious consequences of not believing in what Christ has done for us. 'I wish it could be different,' says Parkinson, 'but if it can't then the warning needs to be taken seriously' (2016). However, we can be set free from the judgement of God, who has no choice but to give the black stone to those who will not believe on His name (2 Corinthians 5:10). Praise God that the death of His Son has removed the black stones from those who run the race and overcome through His strength to finish the race through this world, to reach heaven and God Himself.

The name on the stone would be a new name, one that would describe the person and their character, now like Christ. Alcorn (2004) says that there is beauty in the privacy of knowing something about someone that no one else knows. Only God and you will know what is written on that stone, because in that private part of a loving relationship *we will know fully, even as we are fully known* (1 Corinthians 13: 12).' The Pergamum church had truly run the race, completed it, and kept the faith at the same time (2 Timothy 4:7). No longer was there any guilt or condemnation instead they were completely set free from the law of sin and death (Romans 8: 2).

There is one other explanation of the white stone. In the first century AD a white stone was given to invite someone to a special event – they could only attend if their name was written on that stone which gave access through the doorway to a ceremony or party. We are also invited to a wonderful event, a huge party, in fact it is a wedding. It is our wedding, and Jesus invites us to the feast giving us a very special invitation with our own personal name on it. It is a name that He has given to us – the name by which He has known us since before the foundation of the world, the name that is in His book of life and is there because He died in order that it might be written in blood – His own blood. It can never be erased no matter what we do, because by believing in His name we have personally made the decision to follow Him. Our names are written in the Lamb's book of life (Revelation 20: 15) and we are raised to live with Christ eternally.

Reflection

1. How can you find the courage you need today to witness for Christ in the face of increasing idolatry? Who will you witness to and how are you going to do it? Is your faith and your witness an integral part of your everyday life or do you separate your job from your church and your colleagues at work from your friends in church?

2. Lotz (1997) says that if you go beyond the Word of God you have gone too far. What kind of things are beyond the Word of God? Have you been tempted to justify something in your life which is contra-indicated in God's Word? If there is anyone in your church who is teaching beyond the Word of God, what should you do about it?

3. Satan's throne, which used to stand at the top of the hill in Pergamum has been taken piece by piece to the Berlin Museum and now sits in the centre of Europe as a deadly reminder of the practices for covert and insidious satan worship. What power does Satanic worship still have over our world today?

Amid atheism and secularism that is sweeping across our world, we are called as a Church to arise and put our armour on. Stuart Townend's hymn states firmly where our responsibility lies, it is to listen to the call of Christ our Captain: https://www.youtube.com/watch?v=bQsX8tl9W5Q It subscribes to the call in Ephesians 6: 13-18 to use the full armour of God against the wiles of Satan. As you listen consider how much you use this armour daily.

The letter to the Church at Thyatira

Summary of the letter to the Church at Thyatira

Thyatira's industry was based around textiles, particularly in the making of purple cloth. The unions were strong and dictated not only education for the population but also a social structure to which people were obliged to belong if they wished to further careers and increase their income.

The Christians were often compromised as many of the social events involved alcohol, gambling, and sexual immorality. Yet the Lord praised them for endeavoring to keep their lives pure and maintaining their witness for Him in such a godless and secular society. However, in their midst one person had been given misplaced authority and was leading the church away from the word of God.

This is no different a picture from today where one or two people may be given authority without accountability in the church causing people to compromise their faith and the teaching of the word of God. The church needs alerting to discern false teaching.

Now read on...................

John's memories of the Church at Thyatira

The fourth letter was to the church in Thyatira, the first city that you come to as you turn inland from Pergamum and fifty miles from the coast. We have no knowledge of John visiting this church but given that the apostles wrote letters to the churches and met at conferences, this church must have had some engagement with apostles or visiting preachers.

The letter to the Church at Thyatira

Revelation 2: 18-29 (NLT)

'To the angel of the church in Thyatira write:'

Dear Brothers and Sisters at the church in Thyatira,

'These are the words of the Son of God; whose eyes are like blazing fire and whose feet are like burnished bronze. I know your deeds, your love and faith, your service and perseverance, and that you are now doing more than you did at first.

Nevertheless, I have this against you: You tolerate that woman Jezebel, who calls herself a prophet. By her teaching she misleads my servants into sexual immorality and the eating of food sacrificed to idols. I have given her time to repent of her immorality, but she is unwilling. So, I will cast her on a bed of suffering, and I will make those who commit adultery with her suffer intensely, unless they repent of her ways. I will strike her children dead. Then all the churches will know that I am he who searches hearts and minds, and I will repay each of you according to your deeds.

Now I say to the rest of you in Thyatira, to you who do not hold to her teaching and have not learned Satan's so-called deep secrets, 'I will not impose any other burden on you, except to hold on to what you have until I come.'

To the one who is victorious and does my will to the end, I will give authority over the nations, that one 'will rule them with an iron sceptre and will dash them to pieces like pottery', just as I have received authority from my Father. I will also give that one the morning star. Whoever has ears, let them hear what the Spirit says to the churches.'

With every blessing to the church that I know so well,

Yours in the name and the power of our Lord Jesus Christ,

John

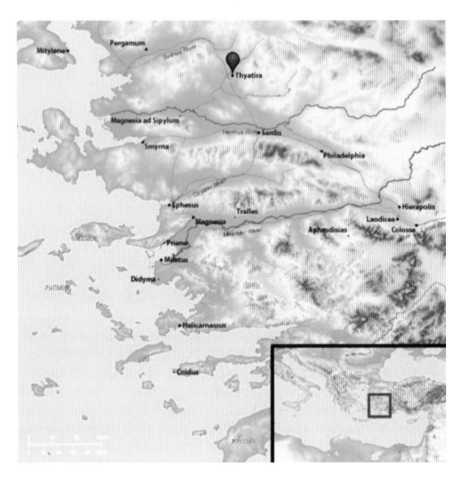

Biblios Maps

History of the city and Church at Thyatira

Thyatira, now known as Akhisar in Turkey, was a church at the busy junction of a Roman garrison and a highway. Although it was small it boasted an industry in pottery and the making of purple cloth from wool, dyed purple or indigo using an extract of shellfish which had made Thyatira well known. Lydia, whom Paul met by the riverside in Philippi, was a businesswoman from Thyatira dealing in purple cloth (Acts 16:14). Those who led these industries were part of a closed trade union who guarded the trade activities with a fanatical possessiveness. No other city in the Roman world boasted as many guilds, hence the very specific difficulties that the church in Thyatira encountered. They had the typical events of unions: dinners and ceremonies which often ended up in compromising situations involving alcohol and immoral behaviour. Christians were caught in the middle as they were taught to behave without corruption, exemplifying Christ. However, if they stepped back from the trade unions they were left without jobs or businesses. There was no focus in this city on any religion, the townsfolk were far more interested in trade and consumer goods.

Message to the Church at Thyatira and application:

There were three main points for the church in Thyatira whose name meant continual sacrifice.

1. They were commended for their works of service which were increasing all the time.

2. The insidious nature of sin caused the Lord to remind them of Jezebel's story or misplaced authority, telling of idolatry, sexual immorality, and corruption in the marketplace.

3. The reward of holding on to the Word of God and recognising who holds ultimate authority.

This small church in a busy and flourishing city does not appear to be a persecuted church, or if it was that did not seem to be the main problem. It stood not only at the physical crossroads of commerce and trade, but also at a spiritual crossroad. If the woman who was labelled Jezebel was allowed to continue in her misjudged and ungodly teaching, then the lampstand from this church would disappear and she would be personally judged. However, if she was removed then the church could continue in its witness for Christ.

Increasing works of service

This church found itself listening to words issuing from the mouth of the Son of God, who did not fail to make His authority and purpose clear in this church. He came to them in awesome power and holy might with His eyes blazing and His feet purifying the very ground He stood upon (Revelation 2:18). Jesus stood looking straight at this church, His eyes on everyone present, searching out those who were harming the vulnerable, the lost and the weak. He saw everything that they did, their deeds of kindness, their patience with the townsfolk with whom they rubbed shoulders; their loving acts of generosity with those less fortunate than themselves including the poor and the widows. His eyes were continually on the righteous, listening to their message of love in a society driven by consumerism and marketing (1 Peter 3: 12).

But as He watched, so His face turned against those who would destroy His church with false teaching. Fire leapt from His all-seeing eyes to consume with a terrible wrath the interloper who dared teach anything other than the Word of God that cuts through bone and marrow, separating truth from lies. As His feet trod the pavement where this Jezebel stood, they became like burnished bronze, which requires melting in a fearsome heat, destroying all impurities. Yet we are reminded, that through those caring, loving, patient feet of our Lord Jesus, went the nails of Calvary. Driven in by the hammers of men who cared not that this was the Son of God who called out from the cross 'father, forgive them for they know not what they do' (Luke 23:34). Despite all the conflict and division that this Jezebel had caused, the Lord Jesus was ready to forgive her if she could only repent of her waywardness and desire for control and power. It was for such as this woman, and us, that Jesus went steadily and lovingly to the cross.

The one who died on the cross came and talked to the church in Thyatira, gently and softly, yet also with loving discipline. He saw what they did, he noted their love for others and their faithful service and commended them. He affirmed their deeds, which every day they continued to do. Perhaps they had soup kitchens or food banks for those that had failed to get into the unions. Maybe they visited the lepers on the edge of the city who once were well known businessmen and traders and were now outcast and strangers. Possibly they visited the prostitutes who had fallen foul of the rich who could afford to pay for any kind of sexual deviation and then throw the girl aside when she became diseased or pregnant. These perhaps were the kind of deeds that the people in the church were doing, often going without to give to others, sacrificing their own food and room in their houses for the homeless, giving of their time from morning till night laboring under the hot sun for the sake of the men and women in their city. These were the ones who were bringing the light of Jesus into a dark world. And the Lord saw what they did, saying, 'well done, good and faithful servant.'

Under the most constant pressure to conform to a godless society, these men and women were walking the city and persevering, finding those who needed the love of God in their lives. They were resilient, committed, passionate and caring, doing more each day as if their strength was being renewed supernaturally. They were living out the words of Paul, 'Therefore, we do not lose heart. Though outwardly we are wasting away, yet inwardly we are being renewed day by day' (2 Corinthians 4: 16). And what was their motive – what could they see that perhaps we can't see when we desire space and 'me time' and rest time? It was in the next verse of Paul's letter: 'for our light and momentary troubles are achieving for us an eternal glory that far outweighs them all.'

The Thyatiran Christians could see something that made them realise there was a better day coming. They were focusing on the beauty that they had found in Christ Jesus and the joy of eternal rest that they had not earned but had been given by grace. No matter what was going on around them, they were faithful and true, giving their acts of service in a pressured society who thought they were old fashioned and moralistically prudish. They had already received a letter from their dearly beloved John who had encouraged them with these words:

'You dear children, are from God and have overcome them, because the one who is in you is greater than the one who is in the world.' 1 John 4:4

Learning to repeat those words when we are under pressure from colleagues or even others in the church are tools given us by a God who cares about our situation. Our God is greater than the plans others would have for our time; greater than the expectations others have of us; greater than those who would seek to bring us down; greater than those who want power and control in our churches at any expense. The Jezebel who represented the world in the middle of the Thyatiran church could not harm them if they kept close to their Lord despite the insidious message she was preaching. For those under pressure today to yield to market forces and a world consumerism which conflicts with the message of Christ, we need to keep loving our neighbours as ourselves, loving God more than our business opportunities and keeping ourselves pure in the sight of God. This message should resonate with a call to do what this church did – to increase our giving and our opportunities to serve. For the One who is within us will give us the strength, resilience, and patience we need to survive where people blatantly misuse the Word of God to justify their own purposes.

Teaching which misleads a church

What of those in the church who are taken in and misled by false teaching? It is probable that the name Jezebel is not the real name of the person causing such division in the church at Thyatira. Jezebel's story is told in 1 Kings 16:29–34 and 21; 2 Kings 9: 30–37. Her life appears to be one of misdirected anger and discontent. She was the daughter of the King of Sidonia, a fierce and committed Baal worshipper. Baal worshippers taught entertainment of the senses, mostly in the form of public sexual acts including the sacrifice of children. All sense of love was corrupted into methods of performance that delighted the masses and hero worship of the entertainers who acted out these dishonouring and disrespectful acts.

Today there are tiny pockets of Baal worshippers who continue to look to Baal to provide them with fertility and rain for their harvests. However, some (Proclaiming the sufficiency of Scripture 2018) would say that Baal worship still exists by another name, through public viewing of sexual acts in films and the rejection of children because of selfish desires of parental needs. Jezebel's worship of Baal resulted in a country that was torn apart by her corrupted worldview, there was no room for love of a neighbour or seeing someone as better than yourself. Baal worship or self–worship gave a distorted view of human society and respect for others. Jezebel lost sight of all that was good and most crucially, she disrespected God who is Lord of all the heavens and earth. Although many prophets came and begged her to turn around and repent of her deeds, and listen to the people's needs, she refused. Even at the end when war was at her gates, she put on makeup and dressed in her best sitting at a window to show her status to the world. Finally, she was thrown out of the window by her servants and eaten by dogs.

Jezebel was the name given to the woman who had taken on practices in the church that was outside her remit as a Christian woman in the fellowship in Thyatira. She was interpreting the Word of God in error but teaching authoritatively so that members of the church were following her word rather than the Word of God. She had brought in a secular and popular message that appealed to those in the church who were either young in the faith or whose own motives needed justifying. There are two questions which we need to ask from this letter. Firstly, what was one woman doing with so much unchallenged authority and secondly, were the elders of the church pastoring their flock as Paul and others had taught them to do?

In the letter to Thyatira the Lord listed the wayward teaching that was being taught in His name, practices that were not only against the Word of God but were directly against all that Jesus had taught them while on earth. These practices concerned sexual immorality, fortune telling and using food and drink in such a way as to cause offense to other members, all under the guise of biblical teaching to justify what was essentially idol worship. Worship in any other form that does not focus on the Lordship of Christ and the reverence and holiness of God the Father is dishonouring to His name and the Lord Himself was calling them, as a church, to account.

So how was it that this woman was able to take on board so much authority that people in the church were swayed by her teaching? Women in general hold enormous responsibility in all areas of life – they are the emotional thermometer for family life, ensuring that all members of the family are cared for in ways that are most appropriate to their needs. It is women who understand and have compassion for those with whom they come in contact. The bible affirms and complements those qualities that are essential to community living (Proverbs 31:10–31). Paul himself continually thanks the women who have cared for him on his journeys (1 Corinthians 16:19; Romans 16: 1,2,6,12). His message to women does not waver across his letters: they have a role to play in the same way as the rest of the body of Christ to work together building each other up (1 Corinthians 12: 12–28). Wives are to respect and love their husbands (Ephesians 5:33) and women are to be reverent in the way they live as an example to younger women in the church (Titus 2: 3). Peter also advised women to be gentle and quiet, pure, and reverent (1 Peter 3: 1–6). 'Jezebel' had missed these important parts of the letters that had been sent to their church. Had she unknowingly missed them or was she interpreting them in such a way that justified her way of living, using the church to give herself the role that she personally desired? It was certainly not the role that the Lord wanted and had prepared for her. Each of us have been given a specific role that builds up the body of Christ, ensuring unity in the church and maturity in Christ (Ephesians 3:12). Jezebel did not want the role that had been marked out for her by the Lord who knew her abilities and skills. Instead she desired what she saw in the city around her – ambition; status; power and control. It was this misplaced desire that eventually controlled and enslaved her, threatening the foundations of the church she wanted to control. When our desires are not in tune with God's plan for us and His church, then we will know by the disunity that surrounds us. At that point we need to ask His forgiveness and let him take back the control we tried to steal.

Necropolis in Western Turkey

What of the elders who were pastoring this church? John, the apostle to Asia Minor, had previously written to the churches a letter that has been brought into the canon of scripture detailing a similar situation. Whether this was to the church in Thyatira or not is unimportant but John, as the writer of love, sent his second letter (John 2) to one lady. This letter details a family that has had many challenges – some have fallen away from believing in the Lord, others have continued. But the lady herself needed that sustainable transforming love that can only come from the Lord. He asks her to remember what Jesus said in his last few days on earth – to love one another. Loving one another enables us to be obedient to His commands, walking in His truths and following His footsteps.

There is no better way to live, for to do otherwise is to deceive yourself and those around you. He commends this lady for having worked for the Lord in the past and having truly followed that sacrificial pathway. But it looks as if she is running beyond the Word of God, seeing thoughts in the bible that are not there and interpreting it in ways that are divisive rather than unifying the body of Christ. Paul's advice to Timothy as a young pastor was that he needed to nurture the courage to teach the undiluted word of God. Deacons were to be men of honour (1 Timothy 3:9) ensuring that the truth of the Word of God was taught, always reflected in the way that they were living. He warned Timothy about the godlessness of the last days and to have nothing to do with those who would try and control others (2 Timothy 3: 6) saying that there would be a form of godliness but lacking the foundation of the truth of God.

The courage to honour God and do what is right often means going against a surging tide of what the world would have us believe is morally good. It seems that the Lord was not going to strive with this woman any further. He had given her time to repent and although the elders in the church should have dealt with the situation, they had abdicated this responsibility. So the Lord himself was going to deal with her and the discipline meted out for this individual was to be an example to all churches. With the demise of this woman the rest of the church could serve God with freedom and joy, holding on to what they already had. This did not mean that they would not love her or care for her – this should continue outside of the church. When Jesus said love one another, love your enemies and bless those who curse you, He meant exactly that. He loves His church, His bride who cost His life, and the message to Jezebel is one of sadness that she could not be a part of that church while tearing it apart by her divisive teaching.

Her future instead now lay in a sick bed with her children dying around her, even though God had in grace and mercy given her time to repent. Not only was her family to suffer, but all those who had come in contact with her were going to suffer intensely – unless they realised the cause of their suffering and turned away repenting to God for their misguided loyalty. We need to be aware of following a person rather than God and are called to pray for wisdom to discern the spirits that we meet; courage to speak out against false teaching; love for our brothers and sisters in Christ, honouring them above ourselves ensuring the unity and peace of our local churches.

This is a warning against harbouring those in the church who would lead members astray. God wants all men everywhere to repent and gives time for these people to do so, but when they refuse there must be discipline for those who have given themselves up to carry out practices which do not adhere to the Word of God. Nowhere does it say that the promise of being the children of God is revoked. We are forever His and only His. God is rich in mercy and slow to anger, but He will not tolerate continued sin in His kingdom. It is for this reason that the churches lose their lampstand and the people causing the dissension or departure from His Word are disciplined.

Holding on

The message from Jesus to this internally beleaguered church came out to them loud and clear, that they were to hold on until He came back. They had no idea when that would be, but the command is sure – no matter how long that takes, just hang in there and don't let go. Don't let go of God, the only One who can give you the strength and courage to hold on despite your doubts and wavering faith. The woman who took hold of the garment of Jesus in the crowded throng had no understanding of what He could do – she had limited experience of His power and authority, yet she hung on to the only thing she could see

(Luke 8:44). She had little left in her life and this was her only chance, so she grasped it and was healed! That is what the Lord asked the Thyatirans to do – hang on and don't let go for their reward was more than they could imagine.

This is the only way to overcome the challenges and difficulties in our lives. To overcome is to succeed and defeat with a power that is stronger than ours – this is what the Lord means. If you succeed in continuing to hold onto Him and don't let go; if you are able to defeat those things that threaten to overcome you; if you have power which comes from Him to go beyond your circumstances, then God will give you authority over the nations in His kingdom. The Thyatira church would have the authority and power that they did not have in the past while on earth. The Lord quoted to them His own words from Psalm 2: 9 which David had written down in a previous millennium: *'He will rule them with an iron scepter; he will dash them to pieces like pottery.'* God is reminding the world that Jesus Christ the Lord is His Son and has handed to Him the inheritance of the whole world. Satan could not ever offer it to Jesus on the mountain of temptation – it belonged to Jesus already. The Thyatiran Christians would be the ones who would be smashing the pots with iron rather than the corrupt trades around them smashing up their wills and grinding them down to nothing.

For us today it is a marvelous thought, that those who are vulnerable, yet love the Lord; those who are homeless, yet love the Lord; those who are hungry and poor, yet love the Lord; those who are meek, yet love the Lord WILL INHERIT THE EARTH! (Matthew 5: 5). Alcorn (2004) says that *'some of the most qualified people to lead in Heaven will be those who don't want to lead now.'* This is the inheritance that we have with our Lord to share for eternity.

It was Irenaeus who said (Alcorn 2004):

'In the messianic kingdom the martyrs will reclaim the world as the possession which was denied to them by their persecutors. In the creation in which they endured servitude they will eventually reign.'

We have an inheritance that as believers in the Lord Jesus Christ, we will inherit along with Him because we are made the children of God through our belief in the salvation and work of His Son. Sharing in His sufferings while here on earth makes us co-heirs with Christ (Romans 8: 16, 17) and therefore inheritors of the glory of heaven with Him.

What of those though, who are taken in by this Jezebel, this idol worshipper and teacher of false ideals? It is possible that her 'children' are those who followed her teachings – perhaps in their ignorance and naivety, and so bear the consequences with her. The Lord said He would strike them dead, because they were sadly misleading the church along with her. We all have a choice to seek the truth no matter what others are teaching and with however much authority they claim it. There was a Pastor who would continually remind his congregation to check out his teaching from the only authority that existed on earth, God's word which was a very courageous act. But he was right, we should not be taken in by anyone, instead wholly lean on Jesus' name, as the old song goes. Jesus is whom we should be continually looking to for guidance and truth in this sinful world that we are passing through. It is so easy as Jude said (v22,23) to be caught up in the fire of corruption, tainting our witness for the Lord and our relationship with God. Jude pleads with stronger Christians to look out for their brothers and sisters, rescuing them from their doubts, fears, and false teaching. But to do that, we must know the scriptures well and ensure that at every point we are not ourselves becoming prey to the false teachings of this world. We need to know what God is saying and are not just being sentimental, or culturally driven, but instead entirely focused on the sharp two-edged sword of the Word of God.

To all peoples the Lord sends a reminder that he searches everyone's hearts and knows who is adhering to false teaching and who is holding on. He knows how to judge between those who can rule and those who cannot. In Alcorn's (2004) treatise on rulership in heaven he says that *'some who are natural leaders here but have not been faithful will not be leaders in Heaven.'* It does not mean that their inheritance of an eternal life will be stolen from them – that came as a gift with their belief in Christ. Some only profess belief with a motive to obtain something else – these God will know all about, for He knows their hearts better than they do. For those who say they are

Christians but in fact are not will be called to the great white throne (Revelation 20:11) and will be judged according to their deeds. God alone is the judge of all the earth (Genesis 18:25) and he will do what is right.

Finally, the Lord will give to those who overcome, the 'morning star.' We are first introduced to the morning star as a plural concept in Job (38:7) where all the morning stars sang together at the commencement of creation. In Revelation (22: 16) the Lord reveals Himself as the 'bright and morning star'. The morning star appears at the blackest time of the night just before dawn breaks. Christ is there with us in the darkest of moments, when we think we are entirely alone, but will disclose himself in the brilliance of light to those who seek him. The person who was there at the beginning of the world now reveals the end of the world and is the only person who has the authority to discipline and reward His own church – the ones for whom He gave His life (Revelation 5: 9,10). He was offering Himself to those who had held on. This is the Christ in His risen and perfect glory, the one who had died for us removing our sins and giving us a glimpse of what is to come. This is the Christ who reveals Himself to the world if they would listen. This is the Christ who is coming in glory for you and for me!

So, what happened to the Thyatiran church in the end? Did those Christians 'hold on' as they were adjured to do by the Lord himself? From this apostolic period until 1922, almost a century ago, the city of Thyatira was home to a Christian community. In 1922 what had become the orthodox Christian population was deported by the Turkish authorities. Today the evangelical link is no longer prominent in this area. Somewhere between then and now the plea from the Lord Jesus to hold on has been forgotten and in its place in present day Thyatira is the unified organisation which calls itself the catholic church. The message to our churches today is to hold on to what we know is right according to the truth of the Word of God. If we can do this then the lamp that we are given to light up the place God has taken us to will never go out.

Reflection

1. Is there a Jezebel in your church today? Do you see any signs of disunity in your church? Is there anything that you are doing in your church which glorifies you rather than the Lord? Are we abdicating our God given responsibilities as Christian men and women in favour of a quiet life?

2. How are we 'holding on' to the truths in the Word of God? Do the doubts and fears in your life cause you to let go of the hand of God?

3. Are you doing as much for the Lord now as you were at the beginning of your walk with Him? Do you have the right motivation to increase your works of service or has it become a load on your back without the joy that comes through knowing Christ?

Suffering comes to us all at different times in our lives as it is part of living in this world. Whatever you are going through at this time know that God is there with you and will hold you safe. Listen to Matt Redman sing the reason why God holds us through the storm: https://www.youtube.com/watch?v=DXDGF_IRJoE   The lyrics in this song echo Psalm 103 which gives us so many reasons for praising God that they cannot be listed. Matt and his co-writer Jonas Myrin also used the 10,000 years of 'Amazing Grace' to show that we need to keep eternity in focus to deal with the present.

Letter to the Church at Sardis

Summary of the letter to the Church at Sardis

Sardis was a city living on its laurels of great wealth mined from seams of local gold, now all empty. Once a great city, it was a place of remnants that could not even keep a trained army.

The church was in a similar state, once running on the love of the Lord Jesus and being the light on the hill, now in name only going through the motions of church life, and all but dead.

The only way to wake up a complacent church that is dying on its feet, is through humility, repentance and renewal which comes from God alone.

Now read on...................

John's memories of the Church at Sardis

The church at Sardis was some twenty miles due south of Thyatira and a similar distance east of Smyrna. These churches would have been visited by Paul on one of his journeys, perhaps the second one which took him along the coast through Smyrna. John may have helped to set up this church and certainly would have written letters of encouragement to the elders there. So as John wrote this short and direct letter to a church in its final death throes he must have felt a sense of sadness and despondency.

The Letter to the Church at Sardis

Revelation 3:1-6 (NLT)

'Write this letter to the angel of the church in Sardis. This is the message from the one who has the sevenfold Spirit of God and the seven stars:

I know all the things you do, and that you have a reputation for being alive—but you are dead. Wake up! Strengthen what little remains, for even what is left is almost dead. I find that your actions do not meet the requirements of my God. Go back to what you heard and believed at first; hold to it firmly. Repent and turn to me again. If you don't wake up, I will come to you suddenly, as unexpected as a thief.

Yet there are some in the church in Sardis who have not soiled their clothes with evil. They will walk with me in white, for they are worthy. All who are victorious will be clothed in white. I will never erase their names from the Book of Life, but I will announce before my Father and his angels that they are mine.

Anyone with ears to hear must listen to the Spirit and understand what he is saying to the churches.'

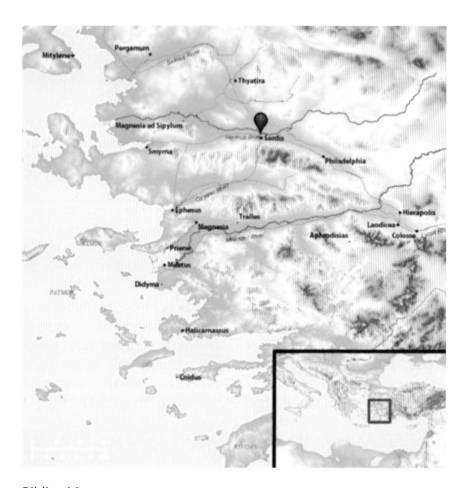

Biblios Maps

History of the city and the Church at Sardis

Sardis means the remnant, the leftovers from a glorious past living on its laurels. This was a complacent church, whose members were living on the fire and devotion of the first few decades, but now only a memory in conversation.

Sardis was one of the great cities in Turkey inland from present day Izmir. It was built on a rich mineral seam at the foothills of Mount Tmolus and the valley of the Hermes River. This combination gave it considerable wealth as the Pactolus Stream bore much gold. The presence of a gold refinery and the first solid gold and silver coins were minted under King Croesus giving rise to the expression 'as rich as Croesus'. Sardis was the chief western terminus of the trade route through Asia and became one of the richest cities of the third century BC. Its main trade was in textiles, jewelry (fire opal and banded agate) and dyes and mined the much sought after blue chalcedony nearby. However, with its surrender to Alexander the Great, their riches became a past reputation and the patron goddess of Sardis, Cybele, no longer brought them success, even though she was the goddess of resurrecting life. With the rise of Christianity, Sardis became one of the main Asian churches with a significant Jewish population, and the largest synagogue discovered of its kind. In 17AD an earthquake hit the city damaging much of their luxurious properties. For the next fifteen years these earthquakes became a regular feature, until finally, in 60AD, a catastrophic earthquake hit the acropolis itself, splitting it into three parts burying thousands of residential accommodation and people (Solomon, 2016). Many of the past architectural glories lay in ruins, still waiting to be rebuilt after previous earthquakes.

The Amphitheatre at Ephesus

The church in Sardis met in the middle of a run-down city once beautiful and rich, now derelict and wasted away. What was happening outside the church had started to become part of the integral makeup of the church itself. The city that was known as the cemetery of a thousand hills (Moore, 2008) stood seven miles away from a huge necropolis where the burial mounds of many thousands stood as a monument to death itself. Sardis was a city going nowhere, dead on its feet, death patrolling the streets in search of forbidden life. The glorification of the deceased within the famous necropolis had insidiously sent tentacles of a creeping necrosis into the corners of the church at Sardis, threatening to pull it down forever.

The textile industry still maintained factories for its famous jewelry made for the tourists, volatile and capricious with no foundation for supporting what was two separate cities built on the mountain and the plain. Even the very name of the sard stones were reflected in the demotivated population of Sardis. Sard stones were a mixture of sard and onyx, flesh toned and meaning claw or fingernail. But the stones were dead, without warmth or vitality, grasping at the edge of reason with fingers that had become fossilized through lack of circulation. Using these stones to carve cameos of life, was all that was left of the ancient city, with a church that had a flickering light in a single window.

Message to the Church at Sardis and application

There are three points which the Lord makes to the people in the Sardisian church:

1. Complacency with lack of insight – what is presented externally is not always what is in the heart.

2. A much needed repentance from this dead existence and to know the beauty of being dressed in white linen.

3. Revival springs from repentance and renewal.

Complacency with lack of insight

There is nothing like waking someone up by telling them that they look like the living dead! A body that no longer has any life left is marble like, stiff and unresponsive to any external pressure; with translucent skin ready to shatter if touched. This was the character given to the Church in Sardis by the Lord who could see into each of their hearts, knowing their deeds and motives. They could have no hidden agendas with Him, and neither could they hide beneath the veneer of outward show. The Sardisian people had a reputation for keeping going despite the odds of which they were unjustifiably proud. Although their city had been devastated by the latest earthquake and there was hardly anything left of the beautiful buildings and the factories that had dominated their skyline, yet they did not let go.

Instead they dressed themselves up with all that they had left, the magnificent jewels, dyed garments, and rich textiles for their houses. Whenever they visited each other they congratulated themselves on what was external. Whether it was envy in other people's possessions or whether it was pride in their own did not matter for it still spoke to them of where their security lay. They had no insight into the awful place that pride had brought them. Rather than trusting in the all providing power of God, they had invested their lives in the transient trappings of external wealth and jewelry. They focused no longer on the saving grace of the Lord Jesus Christ, but rather on the external dressings of a physically degrading body.

It may be that deep down they really were afraid of the future for the city and the church. They were gripped in a spirit of fear that not only paralyzed them but forced them to live a lie rather than admit the state they were in. They had forgotten the words of Jesus that John had sent originally to all the churches:

'I tell you the truth, my Father will give you whatever you ask in my name. Until now you have not asked for anything in my name. Ask and you will receive, and your joy will be complete.'
John 16:23,24

They had no need to fear anything, for the Lord only desired to give them peace and joy out of His mercy and love for them. He did not want to give them the kind of external 'things' that the world possessed, because these merely decay or are destroyed. All the gold, jewels, and rich textiles that Sardis could produce were as nothing beside the peace that He would give. The Lord wanted instead to give them white clothes – a covering of righteousness, cleanness, and purity. The peace which comes with being clothed in sinlessness is overwhelming, taking away the feeling of discontentment and the anger and jealousy of pride; peace which belongs to the Lord Jesus Christ. This gift of peace from the Lord will last forever and into eternity. All the possessions that we accrue while here on earth are worthless not only now but also the minute we draw our last breath and cross over into everlasting life (Matthew 6: 19).

The Sardisians had lost their focus on the future glory of heaven. Instead they looked back and held onto the past in their desperate attempt to retain evidence of past glory. But it was not their glory they should have been focusing on, rather pointing to the glory of their Lord. Down through the portal of heaven the Lord shouted at them in a voice that was like a trumpet: Wake up! Wake up! You are almost dead – can you not see it? The Lord was holding up a mirror in front of them pointing to themselves and begging them to see what He could see.

Being a digital immigrant not very long ago I was stuck in a technology bubble. In my frustration at not being able to make the volume work on my lap top I ended up pressing many keys none of which was responding to my command. While doing this I was speaking in none too affectionate terms to my inanimate and unresponsive machine! It is easy to miss something important, something so obvious that when you do see it, you are angry and frustrated with yourself for your own blindness. We cannot self-righteously point the finger at the Church in Sardis – for in many ways we are like them. Lacking insight about ourselves we think we are courageously soldiering on, yet in ignorance of what is staring us in the face because we don't have time to listen to the Lord who is shouting from heaven. CS Lewis made the point that *"Pain insists upon being attended to. God whispers to us in our pleasures, speaks in our consciences, but shouts in our pains. It is his megaphone to rouse a deaf world."* The Sardis Church suffered from an insidious form of righteous deafness causing a painful numbness in their midst.

A dead person has lost all sense of hearing and seeing, and to rouse the church, the Lord spoke into their death throes and showed them a mirror. This mirror had a three dimensional effect – it showed them what they thought they were like, what they were actually like and what they could become. The Word of God is this mirror, explained James, showing the perfect law that gives freedom (1:25). The Sardisians were chained by their own expectations of what they wanted to be, by what they thought gave them security. But in fact, this existence only served to lock them in a prison of their own making. They had no joy and freedom to leave pride behind them, only a continual seeking after something more all the time and never being able to find it in a city that was itself commemorating the dead.

James reminds his readers, which included this church and us, that we cannot just read or listen to the Word of God. This Word is the living, pulsating, breath of God (2 Timothy 3:16) which strips us of all pretence, showing up every corner of our lives, much of which we would rather remained hidden. But what do we do with ourselves once we see the evidence before our eyes? Rather than ignoring it and behaving as the Sardisian church we need to face the facts as God is presenting them to us. The Church in Sardis was listening to the preaching of the word on a regular basis and were not applying it to themselves at all. They would step out into the sunshine on a Sunday morning and forget everything that was said, running away to buy the latest curtain effect for their house, or the perfume that would make the smell of death go away.

The Lord said to this church, remember the teachings from the Word, do not forget but obey it and repent of this place where you are now, for if you do not, then you will be held responsible for the consequences.

Repentance from a dead existence

Repentance involves looking straight into the mirror provided for us by the Word of God and recognizing that the present way we are living does not meet those requirements. Having seen ourselves as God sees us, we must then be truly sorry for our actions and ask Him for forgiveness. I say the Word of God because there is no other standard by which we can live that is the truth. There are many other ways of living that is morally upright and good, but all of them demand a penance or amends if a person falls short of that standard. Religion demands a standard where the bar is set by humans and therefore fallible. God's standard is so high that it is unattainable for us as human beings. This is where the grace of God saves us. God knows that we cannot be perfectly good – only He is good and if we want to be good we must keep all the commandments as given by Him (Matthew 19:17). Therefore, Jesus came in order that He might save us from our sins and from our inability to reach God's standards. In saving us, Jesus can present us sinless before His Father in heaven and we can live with Him eternally.

True repentance is a process rather than a single step. Having recognised that we are not living up to the standards set by God, we must turn back to ourselves and examine our actions, to see whether we are truly sorry for those actions. If we are, we must decide whether we want to commit ourselves to changing to God's way. True repentance means to make a U–turn in our behaviours and become a new person. How is that possible you might ask? A patient I once saw many years ago, said much the same thing as we sat and talked about his smoking and drinking habits which were slowly squeezing the life out of him. He said, 'How could I possibly change – I would have to be born again.' He did not realise that someone else had made the very same statement some two thousand years ago, but the answer from Jesus is still as applicable today as it was then:

'God so loved the world that he gave his one and only son, that whoever believes in him shall not perish but have eternal life.' John 3: 16

Once we have believed in Him and repented of the sin that made us fall short of God's standards then our salvation is complete in the one who died to make this happen. We are then able to *'put off the old self, which is being corrupted by its deceitful desires; to be made new in the attitude of our minds; and put on the new self, created to be like God in true righteousness and holiness.' Ephesians 4:20*

This does not stop us sinning for we live in a corrupt body that wants to choose wrong instead of right. Paul said there is a continual war at work in our bodies, half of which delights in the law of God and half of which wages war against our minds (Romans 7:23). The Sardis Church was in the centre of a civilisation that was dying on its feet, yet still had to function as a light to that city, left cut in half as it was by devastating features of a natural disaster. We live our daily lives in a world that is corrupt causing us to drift away from the mirror of the word of God. Paul calls us to offer our bodies as a living sacrifice on a regular basis (Romans 12: 1–3). We will continue in our transformation of being more like Him as we turn away from the pattern that this world wants us to follow. This is the only thing that will renew our minds, not mindfulness, which is the current world's way of changing direction; not a new diet that will only change our physical health; nor a self–imposed meditation that will help us focus on something beyond ourselves. All of these regimes focus on our own self–discipline and strength of character. Only God, who set the standards for this world from the beginning of time, can make us anew through the death of His Son and transform our lives to be like Christ.

What happens if repentance to almighty God is not an option that people take? They have, after all, a free choice. For many of the people in the Church at Sardis who were believers yet not living full life in Christ, the Lord said that He would come to them like a thief in the night. The thief in the night comes and takes what you have without asking and gives it to someone else. The Lord will come when least expected and take away the blessings received in Christ.

Sardis was a city that failed to watch, self-assured in its ability to protect the citizens. Twice in the time of its history it was taken over by enemies, who were watching for a way into the almost impregnable fortress. They observed a sentry dropping his helmet, watched the pathway he took to get down and retrieve it, then waited until night and stormed the city – not once but twice. There was a similar story attached to Edinburgh Castle, so Scotland cannot live on its laurels! This was a city that was destroyed when it was not watching. The sentry had dropped his helmet presumably because it was in his hand and not on his head. Our helmet is the assurance of our salvation (1 Thessalonians 5: 8) but we must wear it for it to be effective. In a similar way we must be alert in our churches to ensure that we are not dying on our feet, that we are watching the mirror of God and continually bringing ourselves to Him in repentance for renewal of our minds and hearts. Those who have not made the decision to repent of their sin will suffer the eternal consequences of separation from God.

To make that decision simply means accepting that Jesus is the Son of God and died for your sins, in order that He might present you faultless before His Father in heaven.

Revival

Yet says the Lord, there is a tiny remnant left in Sardis! This mirrors the incredulity that came from Jesus when the Roman centurion, not of Jewish extraction, said that he believed Jesus could perform a miracle but did not feel worthy enough to have Jesus in his house. Jesus was astonished (Matthew 8:10) and commented on it to the Jewish listeners standing around. Here is the incredulous beauty of the remnant, dressed all in white – with no need of external features. Even though they had lived and worked in Sardis, God saw no sin seen in these faithful believers because He could only see the beauty of Christ in their lives. They had not allowed the world around them to soil or tarnish their clothing. They still sinned but recognised their sins quickly enough before it took a hold in their lives. The richness of their lives came from the fruit of the Holy Spirit:

love, joy, peace, patience, kindness, goodness, faithfulness, gentleness, and self-control (Galatians 5: 22,23). This is the amazing grace, that John Newton described, the slave trader turned Christian. This is the one thing that allows us as sinners to come before a holy God with the Lord Jesus at our side. God sees His Son, His only Son who became that perfect sacrifice for our sin and accepts us as the bride of Christ.

This was the precious remnant of the church in Sardis who had held on steadfastly to all that was pure and precious. The Lord does not in any way give them the responsibility for their brothers and sisters in Christ who are choosing to act independently from the whole body of the church. This letter was to be read out to the whole church and so those who needed to wake up heard the message meant for them while those who had not conformed to the pattern of the world heard their message. Am I listening to the message God means me to hear? Those who walk with the Lord are dressed in the white linen of righteousness. Their names are written in the Book of Life along with the names of those who believe in the Lord Jesus and in that saving grace. We are together in the same book with a promise from the Lord that no matter what happens our names will not be blotted out by the horror of our sins.

This is not just for the Sardis Church, for the Lord in His grace and mercy adds that all those who overcome will be dressed in white. Every person who places faith in Him is made worthy to receive these white garments indicating purity and perfect fellowship with Christ. This promise is totally inclusive for *'He who overcomes, like them, will be dressed in white (Revelation 3:5).'* This challenges our often judgmental attitudes which excludes those we cannot imagine in heaven. The paedophiles; the murderers; the slave traders and child traffickers. In fact, anyone who has threatened and abused another human being. Their sin is no more or less than my own single sin which will separate me from God if I have not sought his forgiveness. It is for these that Jesus loved and died so that they could be a part of His bride. The acknowledgement of us before the almighty and awesome God is beyond our comprehension. How could the Lord bring us into the presence of the one who formed the world; who knows and comprehends the mind of man; who orders the places and times of each person who has ever lived and who will live on this earth. Yet God will look at me and at you and say, *'Blessed are those who are invited to the wedding supper of the Lamb!' Revelation 19:9.*

This is the remnant, and these are the ones who will seek revival in the land where they live as they follow the word of God and do his commands. Revival requires courage and strength with a focus on what is to come in heaven. Revival means to overcome the lethargy and spirit of inertia that covers our churches and our land.

The remnant of wine left at the wedding feast of Cana was only a few drops in the bottom of the empty wine flagons – yet to that Jesus added ordinary water and his wonderful grace to mankind, making the best tasting wine ever – it was the wine of heaven (John 2:10). Whoever makes up the remnant, Jesus will make of those people a witness to rise and serve Him in the place He has given them. They will be fit to wear the white clothes and walk with Him. What a glorious thought for those who are struggling in the churches that God has placed them in and who feel that the burden is too great for them to carry.

'God is able to do far more abundantly than all that we ask or think.' Ephesians 3: 20

A powerful book written by Lennie (2016) maps the revivals in Scotland during the last four centuries. Looking at all the places and the route by which revival took place he comes to a staggering conclusion. There are four factors, any of which are needed for revival to take place:

1. Consistent and dedicated prayer from one person or several persons.

2. The consistent teaching of a visiting evangelist who prays and ministers with those Christians in the area even if they are few.

3. The arrival in the area of a young and dedicated minister or pastor or bible teacher.

4. A powerful post–conversion experience of the Holy Spirit in the life of someone who influences others.

Money, technology, permission, skills, and buildings had no effect on revival of the churches. Instead a passion and a desire to preach God's word and make disciples was the only requisite needed. Oh that revival would happen where we are in order that God's glory might be revealed, and that people would come to know the power and the peace that comes through knowing Him as Saviour and Lord.

How does the letter finish? With a glorious welcome in heaven to those who have overcome all the obstacles that the devil has put in the way, these believers will have their ragged clothes taken away and be given new fine white linen! The Lord Jesus takes us and them by the hand and brings us, whoever we are, to the front of the throne room saying to His Father – I died for this person, I love him, and he is mine (John 17:24)!

What happened to the remnant left in this sad city? In the early part of the nineteenth century, Sardis (Sarte), was a place of ruins, home to herdsmen and mud houses. Mr. Pliny Fiske, a missionary in 1820, wept as he read Psalm 74 amongst the ruins:

'Why have you rejected us forever, O God? Why does your anger smolder against the sheep of your pasture? Remember the people you purchased of old, the tribe of your inheritance, whom you redeemed – Mount Zion where you dwelt. Turn your steps towards these everlasting ruins...'

Reflection

1. What do you see when you look into the mirror that God is holding up in front of you as you read His Word today?

2. Sardis Church is described as the church of the living dead. What caused it to die and are there similar reasons why churches today go out of existence?

3. Revival is not about people becoming Christians but rather about Christians themselves finding a renewed excitement and passion for following Christ and going out with the great commission from Matthew 28: 18-20. What can we do to 'strengthen what remains' in our own Christian lives?

As you reflect on the unfinished task that is presented to all Christians everywhere join with this hymn which asks us to go down on our knees and renew that solemn pledge made before the throne of God. https://www.youtube.com/watch?v=aFHdPCNliwM

This hymn was written by Frank Houghton, born in 1894, Stafford, England, who became Bishop in East Szechwan for the China Inland Mission (CIM). In March 1929, during a period of political unrest and civil war, missionaries had been withdrawn from their stations following the martyrdom of 12 CIM workers. The General Director issued a call for 200 new workers to replace them, in order that the Lord Jesus Christ might be made known in that vast country. The Rt. Rev Frank Houghton wrote the hymn for the Annual Meeting in May 1931 and by 31 December 1931, 200 men and women had left for China fully supported financially and prayerfully by churches in Britain.

He said 'The Lord hath done great things for us....be glad and rejoice for the Lord will do great things' Psalm 126: 3 and Joel 2: 21.

The Letter to the Church at Philadelphia

Summary of the letter to the Church at Philadelphia

Philadelphia was a city, like many in this region, devastated by earthquakes. Necessity being the mother of invention caused the architects to develop an innovative design in foundations of their larger temples, thereby saving them from destruction.

But even these foundations were not as solid as those on which the Christians had built their lives and for which the Lord commended them. Despite their lack of strength and confidence in their abilities, the Lord was there to encourage and build them up.

The picture of everlasting life and joy that is given here is one which the churches today would do well to cultivate. It is easy to focus on the here and now rather than on the future which is ours as a hereditary gift from a loving God. For this we need to build the foundations of love which the Lord Jesus freely offers us and look forward not inward.

Now read on...............

John's memories of the Church at Philadelphia

The Church at Philadelphia was the church of the open door, filled with people who had a reputation for brotherly love despite immense suffering and persecution, like that in Smyrna. Paul had been in Ephesus for some three years and had probably been out on trips to some of the other six churches, encouraging and teaching them in the ways of the Lord. They had, like the other churches received letters supporting them in their times of troubles and had been learning together what it meant to love their neighbours as themselves (Ephesians 4:32).

The letter to the Church at Philadelphia

Revelation 3: 7-13 (NLT)

'Write this letter to the angel of the church in Philadelphia.

This is the message from the one who is holy and true, the one who has the key of David. What he opens, no one can close and what he closes, no one can open:

I know all the things you do, and I have opened a door for you that no one can close. You have little strength, yet you obeyed my word and did not deny me. Look, I will force those who belong to Satan's synagogue—those liars who say they are Jews but are not—to come and bow down at your feet. They will acknowledge that you are the ones I love.

Because you have obeyed my command to persevere, I will protect you from the great time of testing that will come upon the whole world to test those who belong to this world. I am coming soon. Hold on to what you have, so that no one will take away your crown. All who are victorious will become pillars in the Temple of my God, and they will never have to leave it. And I will write on them the name of my God, and they will be citizens in the city of my God—the new Jerusalem that comes down from heaven from my God. And I will also write on them my new name.

Anyone with ears to hear must listen to the Spirit and understand what he is saying to the churches.'

Biblios Maps

History of the city and Church at Philadelphia:

Philadelphia, now called Alasehir, is at the foot of a mountain with volcanic cliffs in which have formed large holes called inkwells (Devitt's) which contain within them a substance for making ink. Other specialties of the region are dried sultanas, good wine, and mineral springs. King Eumenes II named it after his brother's nickname Philadelphos, which means the one who loves his brother. Although Philadelphia was destroyed by earthquakes in AD 17 the temple was one of the only buildings to survive through a fascinating model of architectural innovation. The temples were built in such a way as to withstand severe earthquakes. Their foundations were laid on beds of charcoal covered with wool fleeces causing the structure to float on the soil like a raft. Each block was joined to another by metal cramps, so that the platform was a single unit and could not break up. Because of the AD 17 earthquake the Emperor Tiberius relieved the citizens of paying their taxes due to extreme poverty. In their gratefulness they joined with Smyrna, who was also devastated, to build a temple to their benefactor.

Temple foundations at Ephesus

Message to the Church at Philadelphia and application:

Three messages are given to this loving church, the church along with Smyrna that did not receive a warning from the Lord, only affirmation for their love and obedience to Him.

1. Love covers everything we need to sustain life on Earth – the love that flows from the Lord to believers in Him, and from them to all who meet with that love.

2. There is an open door which is opened and shut by the Lord alone.

3. There are rewards that result from obedience to the Lord.

The love of the Lord Jesus for all people

The Philadelphian Church was the embodiment of a loving, outward looking, God focused church. The kind of church to which we would all want to belong. Recently I walked into a church with some friends where an atmosphere of genuine friendship and love pervaded the whole building – it seemed to be built into the fabric of the church. My friends both commented that if they had the good fortune to live in this place, this would be where they would immediately feel at home. What exuded from this church was a love for whoever came to the door no matter their culture, colour, creed or abilities.

Genuine feelings of love for one another exist not only in churches but all around our world – within families; between individual people and towards vulnerable groups of people that need loving care and attention. This love for others is part of our indigenous DNA, created by God from the very first moment man appeared on Earth. It enables and empowers humans to live together with the certainty that someone loves enough to care. However, this love put there in the beginning by God, who made man in His own image (Genesis 1:27) became corrupted by man. God gave man the choice to choose between obedience and disobedience. Man chose to be disobedient and God who is sinless, could no longer be in a relationship with man. Since that time, (Genesis 3: 22–24) history records the corruption of love through stories of war, murder, lies and deceit. Love that looks perfect to begin with crumbles at the edges and unless it is nurtured, affirmed, and tended in God's original way, loses patience, and walks away.

It is God who showed us how to love sacrificially in the form of His Son, Jesus Christ. When we believe in this love and take it into our hearts, it transforms our lives and gives us a new motive for loving others. It is an everlasting spring which never runs dry because it comes from the one whose name is Love. John wrote copious notes about the love of God – he had seen it firsthand through the one he called his best friend, the Lord. He says that we only truly love because of the great love that comes from Him whose name is Love (1 John 4: 16–20).

True love is that which emanates from God, dwells deeply in our hearts because of our belief in Him and in His Son, and then cannot stay still our hearts. It is an ever–moving fluid–like substance, and like the air that we inspire it is expired to all around us. As God gives to us each breath we take, so that love is breathed out to those around us. It becomes part of our nature as Christians to breathe it on all who come in contact with us, whether they want it or not, whether they believe in it or not. Just as it is so easy to pass on bacteria by a respiratory route or by a touch, so without even realising it the love of God is passed between people. This is the deep, heart seeking, soul inspiring love from 1 Corinthians 13 that we learn from God.

But this love is tough for it is never rude or self–seeking; it only ever gets angry if justified and never keeps any record of wrongs (1 Cor 13:5). It never says one single negative word, but only seeks to build up without thought of impatience, unkindness, or envy. This love can only be truly sustained if it comes of God, for all other love is human and susceptible to the corruption that comes from our naturally sinful nature. While faith and hope exist side by side, it is this sacrificial love that upholds both to the very end. This is the love exemplified in the Lord when He went to the cross. The church at Philadelphia is commended because their love for the Lord who died for them had sustained them through their severe trials. Although we do not know exactly what the severe trials were, they had been able to live through many natural disasters and persecutions, continuing with good works showing the love of Jesus to their community.

The Lord in His letter to the church reminded them that He was the rightful heir to the throne of David, both by birth and by law. His journey to the cross fulfilled all the words of the prophets from the Old Testament including the Davidic covenant which said that King David would have an everlasting king on the throne. Jesus was of the birth line of David, and when He stood before Pilate (Matthew 27:11) affirming that He was the King of the Jews He was speaking the truth. Jesus had no choice but to speak the truth for He was *the way, the truth and life* (John 14:6). His was the final kingship of the throne of David and would go into eternity as the King reigning forever at the right hand of God. No one could come to the Father but through Him and through the way that God had prepared since before the creation of the world (Ephesians 1:4). But that journey was full of persecution, slander, torture, and death. It was undertaken only through the love that Jesus had for each one of us, named on His heart as we are with all our sins and misdemeanors. No-one else on this planet could have undertaken that journey for us, only Him who held the key of David, who was in that blood line and yet was also God in human form.

This was the love key that Jesus held in His hand to open and close the doors of churches around the world and the journey of you and me.

The Open Door

It appears that the Philadelphian Church was not particularly large and the people who went there were not of great influence or high standing in the community. Instead the Lord describes them as having little strength, perhaps a group of people who lacked confidence in themselves and who felt that what they did was of no great consequence to the outside world. They went about their business helping many people without commendation or reward. In fact so much so that Parkinson (2016) describes them as an exhausted church, not only from hard work but also from the continual battering of persecution from fellow citizens. As a result, she says, the beautiful care of the Lord Jesus has opened doors for them to go through. Because Jesus Christ holds the Davidic key to the everlasting kingdom and sits at the right hand of the Great throne in heaven, He is powerful beyond all measure. When He shuts or opens a door, no one can change it, regardless of the wealth or power available to them. God knows that we have little strength, but big potential. Our strength is not enough to open a door, so God opens the door for us. He keeps it open for as long as is needed and all He asks is that we walk through that door by ensuring that we obey His Word and do not deny His name.

When the Hebrew family of two million people came to the edge of the Red Sea and were trapped by the Egyptian army behind them, God said, 'I have an open door in front of you, walk through it.' By faith they ran down to the edge of the sea and as they did so a miraculous corridor through the water opened, evidence of the power of God that has been there throughout all times (Exodus 14:21,22). I am sure that as they walked through the Sea on the dry sandy bed they had quaking hearts and shaking knees. When God opens the door, we must use the opportunity He gives us to walk through, even if our knees are shaking. It is the power of God that enables us to have strength we do not humanly possess to approach situations that are out of our comfort zone. For Philadelphia, the open door represented the way in which they could serve Him whom they loved, despite their weaknesses and timidity.

Lotz (1996) suggests that we see various people as 'having the key' to opportunities in our lives. Employers; parents; the bank manager or friends in high places who could open the way for us, and God may well use such people to move us on in the journey of our lives. But they of themselves, cannot and do not open the way. Jesus said that we should ask Him for anything we need, and He will do it (John 14:14). We should not be troubled or anxious about the future, for the peace that He had as He was about to take the final walk to the cross is the same peace He will impart to us (John 14:27). Whatever is through that open door, no matter how afraid we are of stepping through, has been prepared for us and we have been prepared for it by a loving Lord. We sometimes blame people for closing a door that we think should be open, thinking that these people are being obstructive in our lives. Yet we can look back and realise just why it is that a door was closed when the Lord opened another more profitable door giving greater glory to God. Open and closed doors present opportunities for us as Christians to be obedient to the One who knows us better than we know ourselves. Proverbs (3:5) says:

'Trust in the Lord with all your heart and lean not on your own understanding; in all your ways acknowledge him and he will make your paths straight.'

As I write this there is a digger at the front door of the cabin trying to make a pathway through what is essentially nature's dustbin! Huge boulders litter the area, covered by moss. Numerous new saplings have grown up with old trees strewn between them. By the end of the day, the man and his digger had made a new path, straight and boulder free. Our lives are a little like that pathway: scattered with baggage from the past and littered with wreckages of relationships that have gone wrong or choices made in haste. We cannot see through the debris to where we want to go. Yet our Lord says that if we trust Him and not ourselves and acknowledge who is Lord in our lives, He will take a digger and remove all that past debris, making our path straight, and our destination clear.

The Lord knows what we are capable of and understands that we are weak, but when we are weak He is strong. In fact Paul delights in his weaknesses, insults, and hardships for it is then that he can prove the power of the Lord (2 Corinthians 12:10). This power, Paul says (Eph 1:19,20) is the same power that raised Christ from the dead after He was crucified and pronounced dead on the cross. In the same way, Jesus opens doors for us that we have little strength or understanding to open ourselves. All those who have called themselves Christians will one day be exposed as to the true nature of their hearts, and those who have opposed the gospel of Christ will also acknowledge that Jesus is Lord:

One day, every knee in heaven and on earth and under the earth and every tongue will confess that Jesus Christ is Lord, to the glory of God the father' Phil 2: 10-11.

Sometimes we come to a place in our journey when a door appears to be locked. It is our all seeing omnipotent God who sees beyond the locked door knowing whether it should be opened. He also knows when to close a door having opened it for a short time. This is His sovereign prerogative that we, who cannot see into the future, should not question. It was beyond this door that the Lord saw for the Philadelphians and the surrounding district, a time of trial. This was going to test the faith of Christians and not only them but also every person in the world for a specific period. Because God is in control of our world and the kings and rulers of the earth, including all those who sit in governments (Psalm 2: 2–4) He is also able to say to a group of Christians in the centre of Turkey – you do not have to go through this trial. Why them and not us? Because they had endured patiently and with love, and God said enough is enough. It is not for us to compare our trials and sufferings with another, for only God knows what we can personally endure having given us the character of endurance (James 5:11,12). Blessings follow those who endure including the crown of life.

Obedience and reward

The Philadelphian Church understood that to be obedient to the word of God and faithful to His Name was the foundation upon which they stood. Being obedient would hold them together in unity and in peace despite the surrounding fragile geology. They knew the architectural key to their large constructions was to build on a foundation that moved with the tremors, a foundation that might appear to the outside world as shaky and untraditional. But the rafts of charred wood and lamb fleeces had proved their worth in all the natural disasters that had overtaken their city. It is the same with our faith, if built on the solid foundation of the sacrificial act of the Lamb of God, who gave Himself on the cross of wood for us. He is our rock and foundation who holds us through the chaos and instability of the world. Christ is the chief cornerstone (Ephesians 2: 19–22) and because of Him we are joined together as a living temple in unity with one another. We are daily being built into the walls of that temple by the Holy Spirit, in which our heavenly Father dwells.

The Lord promises the Philadelphian church that He will be with them soon and meanwhile they are to hold onto all that they have in Christ Jesus. This for them is the surest way of being kept safe, for no amount of human endeavor, wealth or promises will keep them from the natural disasters or from persecution for their faith. Their reward is to be found instead in the immortality of what is awaiting them in heaven, a crown, and a pillar in the temple of God.

A crown denotes evidence of royalty and a right to reign in a given place or country. It is richly endowed with priceless jewels that have meaning on a global scale. Much skilled work has gone into a crown, with a history that is often timeless. Each has a story of its own and the narrative involves hard won possession, sacrifice in battle and love for a country. To hold fast to a crown means being alert for any who would steal it and wear the crown as a usurper. Satan would do anything to steal that crown from the believer's head and will suggest insidious ideas that will make the crown slip from its rightful owner. So be careful, watching that nothing comes between you and this reward given by the Lord to all those who do as the Philadelphian church did who endured patiently, the road set before them.

Just as a worldly crown has history woven into the fabric and jewels, so your crown will have your own history written into it. It will tell the story of your spiritual journey and how you did not deny the name of Christ, enduring many trials for His sake. It is only the church in Smyrna and in Philadelphia who are given this special promise of a crown – none of the other churches receive this blessing. As every believer in Christ receives everlasting life in Christ, it seems that this promise of a crown is one of the rewards that Jesus spoke of in Matthew (16: 27). One day Jesus will judge all peoples on the earth according to what they have done rewarding them over and above the gift of eternal life. In heaven's sinless society those of us who do not have this 'crown' will look on those who have earned it, knowing the trials that produced this reward and praise the One who gave it.

The temple that the Lord speaks of is that which is described by the writer to the Hebrews. It is the original temple, a pattern of which is given by God on the Mount of Sinai to Moses, in order that the Israelites could have an earthly place where God dwelt, and where they could worship Him. But the true temple is in heaven:

'For Christ did not enter a manmade sanctuary that was only a copy of the true one; he entered heaven itself, now to appear for us in God's presence.' Hebrews 9:24

The temple in heaven will be made up of God's family bringing all the good deeds and services of obedience that they have been involved with on earth. This is what will make up the thick walls, the jewel encrusted fabric of the temple, the golden floors, and pavements. As the writer to the Hebrews commented, this is not a temple made with human hands or resources, this is far greater and far more real than anything we can imagine.

In 1 Kings (7:21) Solomon made two pillars in the temple, one called Jakin on the south side, which meant *he establishes* and a pillar to the north side, which was called Boaz – *in him is strength*. The king stood by these pillars as a position of authority that established the might and power invested in his kingship (2 Chronicles 23:13) where no one could deny his royal place. These pillars were destroyed when Jerusalem fell (Jeremiah 52:17) but were so enormous with the weight of bronze that they could not be properly categorized and so were taken away in pieces to Babylon. In the temple of God those pillars are restored, made of everlasting material and we who believe are those pillars! The King of heaven is standing with the pillars having all the power and authority on earth and heaven invested in the true and righteous one who is above all. The meaning of those pillars comes true – He establishes everything and in Him is all strength. The old pillars of the law are transitory while these immortal pillars are fashioned by grace, moulded and designed by God.

It is hard to visualize our place within this heavenly temple. What will we be doing and how will the skills we have learnt here on earth become useful in eternity? We use the expression in common speech that someone is a 'pillar of society', not meaning a piece of stone in the city centre, but rather someone who is honest, good, full of integrity, someone who can be trusted, holding the community together. In the same way, the Holy Spirit dwells in our hearts the minute we ask Jesus to become Lord of our lives, making it a temple for the Lord (1 Corinthians 3:16). It is the Holy Spirit who prepares us for this transition to the greater temple of God in heaven, showering us with gifts, teaching us the skills we will need when entering that immortal place to become a 'pillar' in the temple of God. It is almost as if God is 'building' us into the place that He has prepared for us in heaven (John 14:2,3).

While we cannot visualize this living temple, Alcorn (2004 p209) says that it would not be surprising *'to find on the New Earth that nations still exist, and kings come into the New Jerusalem bringing tribute to the King of kings.'* He purports that as co-heirs with Christ, believers will have a significant role in exercising dominion over the earth. Whatever we will be doing, it will be in a kingdom ruled by God that is perfect in every way. We as *'priests will serve our God, reigning on earth' (Rev 5:10).* Never again, says the Lord, will anyone have to leave this temple. When invading armies take slaves or make people homeless refugees, this makes them vulnerable and lost. The way of heaven is to give everlasting security and a job that will never see redundancy or retirement.

The final reward to the Philadelphian Church is a position in heaven of security and citizenship. To be a pillar in the temple of God means that we will bear three inscriptions written somewhere on our bodies – the name of God, the name of the new city of Jerusalem and the new name of God. When the priestly robes were described to Moses on Mount Sinai by God, Aaron was to be given a turban made of fine linen made specifically for the High Priest. What was unusual about it was that attached to the front of the turban was a plate of pure gold (Exodus 28:36–38) with a blue cord, on which was engraved HOLY TO THE LORD. This represented the guilt brought by the Israelites when they came to consecrate their gifts to God. We are so sinful that we cannot bring a gift to God without discovering a false motive in our giving. Aaron stood before the Lord as testimony of the grace which allowed the Israelites to give the gift without just judgement. We come before God today, bringing our sin corrupted lives but the price has already been paid through the death of Jesus, making them pure.

In heaven we will bear that name with a wonderful feeling of liberation from all the wrong motives that satan accuses us even though we have been forgiven. The crown or jewels we are given will bear the perfect name of our Father God. In Exodus

(29:6) Aaron's gold plate is called a sacred diadem, a tiara given as a reward for services to the country, a wreath of precious jewels that is set apart and made for an individual because of their service to the king. The Philadelphian church thought that they were nobodies in a kingdom that was being wrenched apart from its very foundations. But during that chaos they held on to what they knew was right and the Lord gave them a glimpse of the reward that was coming. Here in Revelation you and I are given a tiny vignette of what is to come, and the reality will exceed all possible expectations. So, hold on and continue in your hope for it will fix your eyes on the beauty of eternity.

To bear the same name as God means we are His family – the Bible calls it sonship. Every single one of us living on Earth has a desire for security and belonging. A name gives us identity and standing within the community, just as Adam named the woman Eve as the mother of all living (Genesis 3:20). It allows us to be remembered and known by others and it usually means something to those who love us as family or friends. Our identity will not only be singular, but we will bear the name of God investing in us *the riches of His glorious inheritance in the saints' (Eph 1:18).*

The second name is embedded in the new city of Jerusalem giving us citizenship in heaven. And finally, we will have a new name given by our Saviour – which means we are heirs together with the Son of God! I am named in the Book of Life before I was named by my parents for they didn't know what they were getting, but God knew! God has my real name written down and one day I will know that name. My parents gave me a name to walk around with on this earth, which was corrupted by sin, but my true name, the name that God has always known me by is waiting for me in heaven. Perhaps the geographical location of the Philadelphia inkwells meant that there will be much writing of names in the Book of Life, because of the millions of people who will populate heaven!

Philadelphia was a true example of brotherly love and faithfulness. They worked hard to actively show their love to all men, not just to the Christians. The Jews were persecuting the Christians, described as the synagogue of satan, and when Paul wrote to the Ephesians he said that the death of Christ brought people together in peace, breaking down the walls of hostility. As a result *'we become then no longer foreigners and aliens, but fellow-citizens with God's people and members of Gods household.' Ephesians 2: 19*

Hold on, the Lord said to the Philadelphian church, hold on. How they must have rejoiced together as they read these words! What wonderful affirmation of their deeds which they had previously thought poor, unnoticed and ineffectual! Take heart as you read and know that God in heaven notices what you do and already has the delight of planning your rewards.

What happened to the church at Philadelphia? In 600 AD a plaque on a wall in the city centre denotes the place where the Christians met in a large basilica and although this may have become an orthodox church, it still had a reputation for holding to the teachings of the Lord Jesus Christ. We do not know exactly when the Lord shut this door, but it is still a timely reminder to us today that this church with the open door is what we should be like today in our churches.

Reflection

1. How does the love of God show itself in your church? Turn to 1 Corinthians 13 and read through each verse asking yourself if your love for Christ and his people reflects these words. What will you do to learn the art of loving one another? How is your church family like the temporal, heavenly building of the church of God while here on earth?

2. What doors are open in your church that will bring glory to God in your community? Are you stepping through that open door in the power of God? What closed door are you patiently enduring while waiting for God's calling on your life?

3. Do you feel excited about the prospect of being a pillar in the temple of God? How do you feel about having the name of God on your body and being given a new name from the Book of Life?

Laura Taylor sings John Newton's song 'I asked the Lord' (written in 1779) and discovers the challenges in asking. God answers prayer but in doing so teaches us the lessons we still have to learn, employing trials to make us grow.

https://www.youtube.com/watch?v=0cnEDUMfPXs

The Letter to the Church at Laodicea:

Summary of the letter to the Church at Laodicea

Astute banking and an incomparable commercial trade had made this city the richest in the known world. Devastating earthquakes meant nothing to the city who could afford to rebuild itself bigger and better.

This affluence however, spilled over into the church, so much so that they had become no better than the unbelievers around them. Affluence and materialism had taken the place of dependence on the God who would give them everything that money could not buy.

Perhaps this resonates with the Western world culture today. The church has everything it needs so prayer and reliance on God becomes a dry liturgical response. Like the Laodiceans we have lost our focus of the reality of our sin and God's grace, having locked the Lord Jesus out of our churches.

Now read on.......................

John's memories of the Church at Laodicea

The final letter was to the church in Laodicea, whose name means people's rights, the saddest of all the letters both to write and receive. For us it resonates with what we see happening in the church of the Western world. So, it must have been with a heavy heart that John wrote these words to a church that he will have known in his travels throughout the Anatolian Peninsula. It seems that the church at Laodicea was well known for Paul mentions it in his letter to the Colossians. It was 100 miles from Ephesus, across difficult mountainous terrain and a few miles up the river Lycus from Colossae. Colossae, Hierapolis, and Laodicea were close enough together for Paul, when he was writing to the Colossian church to ask them to pass on his letters to the church in Laodicea. His fellow worker Epaphras, who spent time with Paul in prison, was the full-time worker in these three city churches, teaching and preaching the true grace of God (Col 1: 7). He prayed consistently, begging others to pray with him (Col 4: 12) that these churches might remain true to the Word of God and stand firm against the evil workings of the devil. Laodicea was a church that was covered by prayer, teaching and regular communication with the other churches in the district (Col 4:16).

The letter to the Church at Laodicea

Revelation 3: 14-22 (NLT)

'Write this letter to the angel of the church in Laodicea. This is the message from the one who is the Amen—the faithful and true witness, the beginning of God's new creation:

I know all the things you do, that you are neither hot nor cold. I wish that you were one or the other! But since you are like lukewarm water, neither hot nor cold, I will spit you out of my mouth! You say, 'I am rich. I have everything I want. I don't need a thing!' And you don't realize that you are wretched and miserable and poor and blind and naked. So, I advise you to buy gold from me—gold that has been purified by fire. Then you will be rich. Also buy white garments from me so you will not be shamed by your nakedness, and ointment for your eyes so you will be able to see. I correct and discipline everyone I love. So be diligent and turn from your indifference.

Look! I stand at the door and knock. If you hear my voice and open the door, I will come in, and we will share a meal together as friends. Those who are victorious will sit with me on my throne, just as I was victorious and sat with my Father on his throne.

Anyone with ears to hear must listen to the Spirit and understand what he is saying to the churches.'

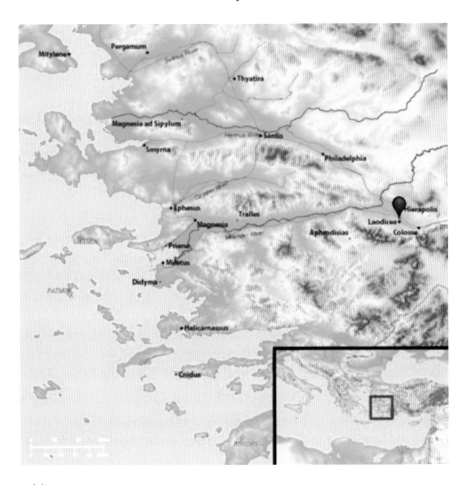

Biblios Maps

The history of the city and the Church at Laodicea:

Laodicea was the richest city with more millionaires than anywhere else in the known world at that time. So rich that when it experienced a horrific earthquake in 60 AD which flattened the city, leaving nothing that was recognizable, they rebuilt it entirely out of their own funds. The Emperor Nero, not known for his kindness or generosity, offered the city charitable aid, which they flatly refused. Their financial wealth lay in astute banking and commercial trade, along with a highly acclaimed medical school which had developed ophthalmic drugs: an eye ointment made from Phrygian stone and ground to a powder. Pharmaceutical companies were rich off the back of medical knowledge. Galen, the famous eye consultant, used this ointment saying that Laodicea was its primary source. The principal deity was Men Karou, the god of healing and agricultural fertility.

After the earthquake which so devastated the city, architects built three theatres with a 30,000 seat circus and a brand new city. The trading centers were salvaged and rebuilt better than they had ever been before and what had previously been Turkey's prominent trade centre now became internationally known. The fine black wool cloth from soft haired sheep was carried all over the world with the result that the exporters became richer and the poor people became poorer, with exploitation of the herdsmen and weavers. Beggars tripled in number as it became the city where money was thrown to the poor and as the city descended into a consumer driven society, so the church followed in its own accumulated wealth. It was into this situation that the letter from John arrived in approximately 96 AD. It must have been a bit of a shock to see themselves described as 'lukewarm' with the potential to make people feel physically sick at the sight of so much arrogance and self confidence in a morally dead society.

Lukewarm was no idle description either. The water that was

pumped down to Laodicea came from the hot springs further north which flowed into the Aegean Sea. By the time it reached the sea the water was cold, but drinkable. In Laodicea however, it was lukewarm and totally undrinkable, in fact it made the consumer sick and was used as an emetic. It was far removed from the refreshing cold water of Colossae or the healing hot springs of Hierapolis. Roman engineers designed vents in the water system so that the pipes could be periodically cleaned of mineral deposits causing blockages.

Paul had a heart for the triad of churches, Hierapolis, Colossae, and Laodicea, visiting as regularly as he could, praying for them all without ceasing (Colossians 1:9). It is possible he never actually met with the believers in Laodicea (Colossians 2: 1) but perhaps some of them came to hear him teach at the Colossae Church for he had a relationship with one of their workers, Epaphras, who also taught in Hierapolis (Colossians 4:13). Epaphras was a hard working prayer warrior and committed in the long term to pastoring and ministering to these three churches. The church in Laodicea was a house church, meeting in the home of Nympha (Colossians 4:15), and they were certainly active in the early days, receiving letters that Paul wrote to them. The Laodicean Church, however, was now in trouble. Having been a lively house group that had full time workers, men and women who were sending and receiving letters from the apostles, they were now floundering on a sea of lukewarm contents of the stomach and likely to be vomited out.

What had happened to this vibrant church that appeared less resilient than the previous generation and unwilling to compromise their worldly lives? Perhaps they were worried for their children's sakes and did not want to be persecuted for their faith or simply had lost the original message as they embraced the world around them.

Message to the Church at Laodicea and application

Three main points come to light here that we will discuss, although there were many other lessons for the Laodiceans to learn from the Lord they said they loved.

1. The blindness that comes from arrogance and pride.

2. The lukewarm character that comes from sitting on the fence.

3. The loving discipline that emanates from our Lord Jesus Christ.

Blindness from arrogance and pride

To be a Laodicean meant that you understood your rights as a citizen of the world, for the city's name meant people's rights. They thought that there was nothing they could learn, for they were the centre of excellence, had earned their money through wisdom and knowledge, healing most diseases particularly those of the eyes. Nobody else had their understanding in financial matters and nobody else could turn stones and black cloth into money. Yet they had achieved this through their own business acumen and even when a natural disaster threatened their whole existence, they were able to turn it around into a business venture. The church had become part of the city around them, with no difference between the world outside their door and those inside who followed God. These were the followers of Christ who were supposed to have the love of the Lord Jesus in their hearts shining like a light in the greed and rights driven society of Laodicea.

Into this atmosphere of self–love and self–righteousness stepped the one who called Himself the Amen. This One was the only faithful and true witness of life itself and ruled God's creation. There was no room for selfish ambition or pride in what they had achieved. The Lord they said they believed in had given up the glories of heaven which was far beyond any of the riches that Laodicea could produce. He had gone to the cross for the very pride that they now displayed because they thought

163

they could manage their own lives. How often do we let pride get the better of us, thinking that we alone can manage, build palaces out of disaster, and control the idols that threaten our existence?

To be described as a disgusting emetic would surely make the Laodiceans look carefully at where they had come from and where they were going. Apparently not as we shall see later. They were so steeped in their own pride and confidence at their great wealth that they were indifferent to the plight of Christians around them, the poverty of other suffering churches and the terrible torture that was being inflicted on their brothers and sisters in Christ in cities around them. Both Smyrna and Philadelphia were on their knees and yet there is no sign at all of help being offered from this overly rich and complacent church. It was true that they were doing some deeds, although these are not recorded as being good. What did they consist of? Perhaps they were offering their church to be used for community entertainments; giving money to vulnerable groups in the city; organising a social coffee morning or a street event.

Jesus looks at them and wants to spit the rubbish out of his mouth. This is social Christianity at its worst, with no thought of the love of the Lord Jesus Christ that spread itself through the community as salt and light, accepting persecution, angry taunts, and ridicule, because they held to biblical standards. There was no persecution, instead the church was as much a part of the city as the city was part of the church. Jesus said to his disciples, *'No servant is greater than his master. If they persecuted me, they will persecute you also.'* (John 15:20) In other words expect persecution at some point in your life, for you cannot say you are the servant and not have the same treatment meted out to you as your master. Every other church around them was experiencing torture for their faith, yet the Laodicean church did not seem to think that they were the odd ones out. Instead, it seems that they were so proud of their situation that they thought God was blessing them because of their financial prowess. Yes, indeed they were being blessed, but in such a way as to enable them to help those in the cities around them. They could not claim ignorance, for Epaphras was working with them and in Hierapolis and they were receiving letters from each other detailing the hardships. Paul was in prison, as was John, yet certainly Paul had not received any monetary gifts from the Laodiceans (Philippians 4:15) who could easily have spared money for his needs. Paul passed on a saying of Jesus which was that it was more blessed to give than receive (Acts 20: 35) yet in Laodicea it seemed to be all about receiving what they felt belonged to them by right.

It is so easy in our western culture to be more concerned with what we are owed by the state or by society than with the prayer of the Lord which said give us this day our daily bread (Matthew 6:11). We need no more and no less than the requirements of a single day which God has promised he will provide. He tells us not to be afraid because it is his perfect love that casts out the fear of anxiety, the fear of going hungry or homeless and the fear of being the one who will stand out (1 John 4:18). Giving produces many godly characteristics for it makes us rely on the one who will provide. It produces patience, to wait for what we need rather than want; it produces courage to face each new day in the strength of the Lord rather than in our own strength; it produces humility, making us rely not on our own resources but on the immeasurable riches of Christ Jesus.

In their arrogance, the Laodiceans thought that their occasional giving to charity and their 'Christian' social and moral deeds would be enough for the sacrifice that God asks of those who follow Him. But He requires much more than that. To give a little that does not make a dent in the bank balance or is not encroaching on personal time and space is not the sacrificial giving required by the Lord. When we become believers in the Lord Jesus, His overwhelming love and our thankfulness at His own sacrifice is the pure motivating factor for going beyond the moral norms. King David recognised that God did not want the outward show of giving, He wanted a servant's heart, whose desire was to follow the will of God and His commandments (Psalm 40: 6–8). Solomon his son, who had learnt at the feet of David, said that it was far more acceptable to do what is right and just than to bring an offering which meant nothing, especially to those who had much and were giving out of their reserves, rather than their only means (Proverbs 21:3). Hosea the prophet, speaking the words of God to the people of Israel, acknowledges the mercy of God for a sinful people was more important than making an outward show of giving (Hosea 6:6).

Corrie Ten Boom, a remarkable woman taken as a prisoner of war during the 1940s in Germany, gave the rest of her life travelling the world to win souls for Christ. One trip in the later years of her life showed just how much of a servant heart she had that went beyond any normal social good. She was in Vietnam having taken a plane across dangerous waters, knowing at any moment they might have been shot down. She was tired when she got into the plane and after two hours she felt as if she had crossed the border of her physical abilities. Getting off the plane she felt worse and could hardly stand but as she looked at the faces around her she experienced the deepest sympathy and love for the Vietnamese. She recognized what Jesus did for her on the cross and felt honoured that she too could suffer a little. She read from John (7:37) *'If anyone is thirsty, let him come to me and drink. Whoever believes in me, as the Scripture has said, streams of living water will flow from within him.'* At this her strength revived and she was able to continue her trip without self-pity and with joy in her heart at the streams of living water flowing from within her because she was connected to the source (Carlson 1983).

The Laodiceans had become disconnected with their source of living water. As soon as our focus is directed away from Him who can provide us with His strength then our human weakness becomes apparent. The living water within us becomes stagnant and lukewarm, no longer fit for human consumption, in fact toxic to health and life.

Perhaps in their arrogance and pride, the Laodiceans were blind to themselves. Despite their world-famous remedies that could make them see, they carried on with the external creams and ointments that would do nothing for the blindness in their hearts. We must examine our own hearts daily to ensure that pride is not sneaking in by another name. It is an insidious evil that causes a barrier between us and the God who saved us. We cannot afford to be proud when there is nothing we can do to save ourselves. Not all the wealth that this world can give could possibly save our souls from an eternal death. Only the One who died that death on Calvary can save us and give us the resources we need to continually offer ourselves as living sacrifices to the world around us.

Sitting on the fence

But it could have been so different. The rest of the churches presented such a different picture of affirmation for their good deeds and counsel on the difficult situations that they found themselves in. The Laodiceans, in their effort to be all things to all men, were in fact sitting on the fence of diluted spirituality in order to remain popular. Instead of being ready to sacrifice their riches and reputations for the sake of Christ they played games in the church pews. Whatever the city said, they went along with the same philosophy and were careful in their relationships to neither upset or overhelp anyone. Instead of following God's commands to make sure that the church was a giving and discipling church, teaching everything that the Lord had commanded them, they diluted its effects.

It is easy to compromise our faith as perhaps the Laodiceans did by giving just enough so that it looks as though the poor are being sufficiently cared for; or giving someone a lift when there is time to spare; attending the bible study or prayer meeting when it is suitable or there is a good speaker; practicing sexual morality until a marriage breaks down and then justifying an adulterous relationship; loving those who are easy to love and forgetting the enemy next door. They had become like the dreadful water that came down the pipes into their houses. Fit only for spitting out, they were full of the poisons themselves that were clogging up their heart systems.

What are we teaching within our churches – is it a dressed down message that is palatable to the listeners, in order that our churches are filled with happy people? It is so easy to desire a church where every pew is full and there appears to be a worshipping audience who 'enjoy' the message. But is that really what we want? Do we really want a social get together of our 'pals' to make us feel good? This is surely only entertainment that ensures the masses are kept in a nice apparently warm state. The Lord said this is not the way to worship Him. For when we do not like the entertainment it becomes easy enough to move on, but worship of our precious Lord Jesus is never entertainment. Without commitment to His Word and a full understanding of what His will is in our lives, we have no need to be accountable to Him as Lord. When we are challenged in our way of thinking, perhaps by the sermon or by our brothers and sisters in the church, we need to take notice of what is being said. It is not easy to speak out and give thoughtful advice when we also must ensure that the mote in our own eye is out first. When the going gets tough and people throw taunts at your faith or despise your adherence to His Word, praise God that you have been chosen to be His servant and are recognised as a child of God.

The meeting in the church that is least attended is always the prayer meeting, yet this is the one place where we bring ourselves before the one who is the object of our affection in order that He speaks His will into our hearts. Pawson (2011) says that 'live prayer meetings only exist where you feel you need God'. It is this meeting that is the powerhouse of the church. Those members who think they can cope without this meeting or say that they can pray in their own homes are deluded by the one who is full of lies. Corporate prayer brings together a church in all its weakness; sadness; skills and strengths. It encourages and unites (Hebrews 10:25) *'spurring one another on towards love and good deeds.'* Without prayer, the body of the church becomes weak, discouraged, and disunited. The Laodiceans did not feel that they needed God, they could cope on their own without any help from Him. But if we do not need God then He no longer has any need of our input into His work.

In sitting on the fence and not taking the commands of God seriously our Christianity becomes what Lotz (1986) calls 'a holy hobby'. We don't let it change us or rock us, we just go with the flow doing what we want to do. Until that is, the Lord comes and stands among the lamps of our churches to discipline our flawed ways of thinking, removing that lampstand if necessary.

Loving Discipline

God was still prepared to forgive them and make them into a working church if they would only recognise their sin turning back to Him. He wanted to come into the church through the doorway for He was not going to come in any other way, He wanted to be seen coming into the church. He wanted to be invited into their homes, their meals, their lives. He wanted them to exchange the frantic trading of their famous black cloth for the white clothes of righteousness; the true riches of heavenly gold which would gild the insides of their hearts rather than the outside of their temples and homes; exchange the raking in of money from the pharmaceutical companies for the gentle cleansing ointment from the hand of God which would heal their souls making the scales fall from their eyes enabling them to see the corruption all around them.

This did not necessarily mean a finish to their trading, but instead it meant a different approach. All that they did would be 'as to the Lord' (Colossians 3:23) and not for themselves. The accumulation of wealth would be for use in the Lord's service, to help other churches who were in dire need. As the Lord had given them great riches so they would be funneled out to those in need, without siphoning off monies because they needed a new fountain in the courtyard, or a new kitchen which they had replaced last year. The Lord wants to bless us and not to harm us (Jeremiah 29:11). He has the overall picture and knows the needs of others which He lays on our hearts in order that everyone would have everything in common, sharing as each has a need (Acts 2: 44,45). If we shared all that we had like that first church in Jerusalem no one would have any need and our churches and communities would look entirely different as a result.

In Keble College, Oxford, there is a picture painted by Holman Hunt in 1853 of the Lord standing outside the door of the church, knocking sadly, and waiting for someone to get up out of their seat and open the door. Hunt started this painting when he was 21 years of age but did not finish it until he was 29.

He had been looking for a perfect representation of the dawn which just shows in the distance of the picture. Eventually he found it when visiting Bethlehem and saw the perfect dawn over this little town. I must admit, that although I have seen this painting many times I have never seen the dawn until I sat down to write about this letter to the Laodiceans. Somehow it shows my own blindness in that something we think we know so well, is showing us a message that it has long been sending. The two lights in the picture represent conscience and salvation. The rusty nails and hinges show a door that has long been closed and is almost impossible to open. The only access is from the inside as there is no handle in evidence on the outside. Perhaps the door has never been open and in fact some commentators do hypothesize that many of the Laodiceans were not Christians at all. It was for them an exercise in social responsibility. Either way, the Lord is offering them another chance to repent and change their ways, becoming a working part of the body of

Christ. He loves them but is not allowed into their church and it is their responsibility to invite Him in. They can change, for the existence of the new dawn in the picture gives a ray of hope amongst the fallen fruits of Autumn. The Lord says you CAN become rich in things other than worldly wealth which is merely mortal; you CAN cover yourselves with the white robes of righteousness rather than the black wool of worldly fashion which will change tomorrow; and you CAN be given a medicine of God which will open your eyes and make you see His beauty and grace towards you.

This is the discipline of God – He refines us in the fire to become like gold making us more like Him, so that we will represent His truth, and glorify His name. But if we try to dodge hardship by making ourselves comfortable then we lose the delight of becoming like Christ.

Holman Hunt 'Light of the World' Keble College Oxford

The Lord's final plea to the Laodiceans is that the rewards He offers far outstrip anything that they could possibly earn through their dealings in the business world. Nothing can measure up to sitting with the Lord in eternity, reigning with Him. There is proof of this from His resurrection and subsequent ascension into heaven. The angels said to the Laodicean church *'in the same way that He ascended to His father and sat down at His right hand, so will they'* (Acts 1: 9) if they overcame the collusion that they had with the world.

The Lord gives us every opportunity to repent of the direction we are going if it is away from His commandments. It is easy to fall prey to the temptations that satan offers us, a bigger house, because we need it, a greater income, because we need it, greater academic status because it will help us develop our understanding. But what the Lord gives is of far greater worth when He can see the eventual outcome and it may be that on the way He will bless us with these material blessings which are given to be used for His glory.

'Repent before your lamp stand is taken away from you and given to another, says our gracious, long suffering and merciful Lord, for I stand at the door and knock. If anyone, anyone at all, is hearing then please open that door' (Rev 3:20). Our Lord is merciful to all and if there is a church who has lost its vision and their spiritual temperature has grown cold, then it only needs one person to pray and God will heed that prayer. Perhaps you are struggling in a church that is more world focused than God focused. Perhaps you feel isolated in your heart as you think that maybe you should move from this lukewarm church. But God is refining you and desires that you stay and pray, leaning on Him for every step and strength to carry on His work in the place He has given you until He removes you.

John in his sadness may have wondered if he could he have done anything to stop this capricious and insidious slide into indifference and decay. Should he have been more courageous in his discipline of the church as an apostle of Jesus Christ? It is easy with the benefit of hindsight to wonder if there was anything we could have done differently. The truth of the matter is that each one of us is responsible for our personal relationship with God; no one has the responsibility for another man's heart. Church leaders are responsible for leading their flocks on the right pathway that is consistent with the Word of God. They will have their own discipline to bear from a Holy God if they are only pretending to do the job to which they have been divinely appointed. Woe betide those who are either ministers or pastors and are not believers, or those who say they are believers and are not preaching the truths of the inspired Word of God. As we said earlier it would be better if a millstone were tied around his neck and he were cast into the sea.

Natural deposits from the earth near Heraclean Western Turkey

There comes a time when the warnings from our Lord have run their course. A few years after this letter was received, a second earthquake buried Laodicea and it has never revived. Nothing is left of the church that thought it was invincible because of riches and reputation. Jesus himself had sent them a letter which they ignored, and they bore the consequences of refusing to repent and turn again to the God who had given them everything they owned in the first place. He had gifted them with riches to share with other churches and their brothers and sisters in Christ, but they chose to keep them close to their chests.

'Whoever finds his life will lose it, and whoever loses his life for my sake will find it.' Matthew 10:39

Since the second world war, our world culture and social behaviour has changed dramatically. The church is no longer considered a higher authority, but perhaps it does not deserve to hold this right. God's name is used often as a swear word or inappropriately in conversation and bible teaching, especially biblical prophecy, has been largely abandoned by the formal church.

We have become lukewarm – a temperature that is so bland it makes the author of life want to spit us out. The cause of this bland society can be found in people's choices. Materialism is a sacrifice to the personal ego and status. This digital age which could be and sometimes is, used for God's glory so often takes the place of God in our lives. Moral and ethical structures are covered up by messages which seem to say we care about one another. Charities abound, and the ecological structure of the earth is being considered as never before, but what is man really aiming for? Is it about others or is it about himself? Equality and diversity of our society allows the justification of any type of human state because people no longer fear the Holy God who sits on the throne of judgement. Instead, every man does what is right in his own eyes (Judges 21: 25).

However, for those who do see the sin in themselves and repent, Jesus is ready and waiting to forgive immediately, for He is standing right at the door. For those who believe and overcome this state of soul apathy, a place in heaven awaits with Jesus Christ to reign forever with Him.

Reflection

1. The writer to the Hebrews (12:11) says that 'no discipline seems pleasant at the time, but painful. Later, on however, it produces a harvest of righteousness and peace for those who have been trained by it.' Do you see any situations in the church or in your life that you would describe as discipline from God? How did you deal with being disciplined and what was the outcome? Has reading about discipline in the Laodicean church changed your opinion on the subject?

2. Is the way that we live as Christians in our communities affecting those around us? Does the teaching in our churches challenge us regularly, making the church a focal point as a faithful and true witness to the Creator of the Universe?

3. Is God asking you to be courageous in a church that has become lukewarm and has lost its sense of direction from the word of God? What is your own spiritual temperature like and how can you increase it to make a difference in the community where you live?

May the words of Keith Getty and Stuart Townend's song 'Holy spirit living breath of God' breathe a spirit of revival into your heart and soul. This is the final hymn they wrote together on the Apostle's Creed Album focusing on the basic tenets of the Christian faith. Our faith must connect with our daily lives otherwise it is meaningless. Daily we need to pray that the Holy Spirit transforms us from the inside to love and treasure God's word and His ways. 'Only through reaching the end of ourselves can we achieve a vibrant Christian witness that everyone on the outside can see as different.'

https://www.youtube.com/watch?v=8nbMfLQd2P4

Chapter Six
Overview of the seven letters to the seven churches

God's message to five of the seven churches is unmistakable – to keep their witness they would have to recognise the decline that they had fallen into and repent, asking God's forgiveness for their arrogance in not seeing where they had fallen. If we want revival in our churches today, we need to look at ourselves and see our desperate state; repent and turn from our indolent ways. Andrew Murray, the great prayer warrior of the nineteenth century, points to sin as the only reason for decline and the responsibility of the church to bring people to repentance:

'Until those who would lead the church in the path of revival bear faithful testimony against the sins of the church, it is likely that it will find people unprepared. Most would prefer to have a revival as the result of their programs and efforts. God's way is opposite. Out of death, acknowledged as the wage of sin, and confession of utter helplessness, God revives.'

The meaning of the names of the seven churches looks like this:

Ephesus – Desirable

Smyrna – Myrrh

Pergamum - Marriage

Thyatira - Continual sacrifice

Sardis - Remnant

Philadelphia - Brotherly love

Laodicea - People's rights

We (Ephesus) are so desirable in God's sight, that He gave His only son to be a sacrifice (Smyrna) in order that we might believe in the Lord Jesus and become His bride (Pergamum). As a result of our belief in Him, we will never perish (Thyatira) but have eternal life, even though we are so much in the minority (Sardis). We are to love one another (Philadelphia) as Christ loves us rather than the inward thinking that only results in selfish ambition and desire (Laodicea).

The two churches whose concept of following Christ were at opposite ends of the spectrum were Philadelphia and Laodicea. Philadelphia knew that they were saved through the grace of the Lord Jesus Christ in their weakness. Whereas Laodicea boasted in their wealth which they believed made them strong. Parkinson (2016) takes the view that all seven churches were facing different stresses and temptations, but their attitudes to those challenges differed immensely. 'The way we live together matters,' not only for the churches themselves but for those who are watching a living testimony to the Lord Jesus.

These letters are included in the Book of Revelation in order that they and we might prepare for the dreadful day of the Lord – dreadful for those who do not believe His message of salvation, but joyful for those who believe in His name. For those churches, whose members are living a life that glorifies themselves, Jesus has a warning which if ignored will remove them from that place of witness to which He has entrusted them. We must choose to examine ourselves, losing our lives for His sake and becoming more like Christ as we die to ourselves and live for Him. The whole of Revelation is based on a feeling of urgency. Jesus came to deliver the message himself for He knew the difficulties and challenges that were being presented to these churches. He also knew that some of those problems could be rectified by reassessing an attitude of lethargy and waking up to face the wiles of satanic activity. *The time is near, John was told at the end of the vision, I am coming soon (Revelation 22:10,12).* This message has been available for the last 2,000 years translated in hundreds of languages all around the world across different mediums of communication. There could not be a greater advertisement for man of God's intent. Yet we insist on ignoring this letter from the God who cares far more than we deserve.

Jesus walks among our churches seeing what we do, removing some from their place of witness, exalting others with His name as the highest name. It is a reality we cannot ignore. In Exodus (25: 31-40) God gave Moses the exact pattern for a lampstand in the tabernacle in the desert. This was a copy of the lampstands that are in the heavenly places (Revelation 1:12). It was to be made of 34kgs of pure gold with almond blossom and buds at six ends of the branches and one for the stand. Almond blossoms appear on the tree before the leaves are produced, which could hide the beauty of the blossom. There is to be no hiding of the light that will emanate from the burning oil, these lamps are for a purpose, to show the world who we serve and the truth of the Word of God. Each blossom forms a cup, and, on the lamps, this would catch the oil so that nothing is wasted.

God never wastes a single drop of Himself in this world. When we come to Him in our weakness asking forgiveness for the misdeeds of our past, He is faithful and just to forgive us our sins (1John 1:9) using us to further His kingdom. But almond blossom has a weakness. It is one of the first to emerge each springtime and is therefore susceptible to frost which will blight the crop. If we become cold to the delights of the Lord by missing our quiet times with Him daily; by refusing to have fellowship with other Christians because so much else has crept into our lives; by forgetting to pray and have that regular conversation with Him; by not seeing the sins that we are committing because we have become so inured to His commands, then we will not blossom as His children. Instead our growth will be stunted, corrupted, diseased, and sometimes die.

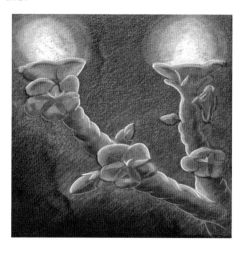

Almond blossoms are best eaten indirectly as honey which gives a beautiful aftertaste, sweet and strong. King David knew what this tasted like when he said:

'The ordinances of the Lord are sure and altogether righteous. They are more precious than gold, than much pure gold; they are sweeter than honey, than honey from the comb. By them is your servant warned; in keeping them there is great reward.' Psalm 19: 9-11

How much more delightful to us is the Word of God than this wonderful honey flavour from the almond tree which is the first fruits of spring? But we must 'eat' of it to be both warned and rewarded. The lampstand in the temple required a constant supply of oil to keep it burning throughout the night. We are living in the night in this world, for it is dark with the deeds of people who constantly and consistently fail to meet the standards required by God to come into His presence. The light of the lamp in the darkness shows up the world's sin and although the world hates to be told of its sin and persecutes those who keep the lamp burning, we are to continue telling the message of God. To do this we need to know the word of God ourselves to answer for the hope that is in us and to do so with grace (Colossians 4:6).

The oil provided by the people of Israel (Exodus 27: 20,21) was to be crushed olive oil, pure and clear. In the same way we in churches must supply the oil for the church to function as a lamp in its community. It is no good closing the door and leaving Christ on the outside while inside is all cosy. We are not to be an entertainment for the community. We are instead marked out to be different, to stand out, be bold and courageous showing people the love of Jesus, but also live by the biblical standard and pattern that have been set by God. The church cannot have that testimony if the people who go to it do not supply the oil. We must supply the oil together for it needs to be brought by all the people as the whole body of Christ (Ephesians 4: 16). The richness of the oil will be seen in how bright the lamp burns – it works better and for longer if the oil is of good quality. It cannot be done by the elders or by the minister – they are guiding the church, the church itself needs to bring the oil allowing it to infuse the pews of the people who are curious and tend to the needs of the fellowship.

Recently I attended a charity function raising money for a respite home in Inverness. There was a wonderful representation of musical skills and ability from across the city, but the most beautiful gift was brought by the Rainbow Choir: a group of adults with additional needs who had been trained by a passionate and committed lady. They sang with utter abandonment, enjoying every single second that they were on the stage. Their feelings of joy and gladness reverberated around the auditorium like refreshing rain, pouring down on the faces of the listeners. Their rainbow T-shirts and beaming faces articulated for them the words that some could not speak. They signed the songs with passion and a deep hunger for something that we could not see. They sang without any shyness or timidity, purely for the joy of singing and exulted in the audience's wondering appreciation. And their first song? Give me oil in my lamp keep me burning! I cannot write those words without feeling a wonder and a tearful emotion that God brought these marvelous people to teach me a lesson of thankfulness to a God who loves me and cares for me.

How can I not bring the best of oil to keep that lamp burning in my church? How can I fail to come to my God every day and talk with Him and walk with Him as I travel this dangerous journey in a dark world? I need Him with me all the time to keep my thoughts, my mind, my heart safe as I step out to do the work that He has sent me to do. The question is – do you?

'For you were once darkness, but now you are light in the Lord. Live as children of light, for the fruit of the light consists in all goodness, righteousness and truth, and find out what pleases the Lord.' Ephesians 5: 8-10.

As you reflect on all that you have read and seen through the eyes of faith, take time to listen to the following song. We can only imagine what it will be like to stand in front of the one who came down from the riches of heaven to die for us sinful being and destroy the curse of death. But as we imagine we can praise and worship Him who died and was raised again for one day we will be there with Him. https://www.youtube.com/watch?v=fLNvHIWVnpE Jesus is our hope in life and in death, nothing and no one can change this fact, for it is not our own hope it is the glorious plan of our Holy God for us.

Bart Millard wrote this song years after his father died. He had been brought up in an abusive home alone with his father, struggled through a lifetime of guilt and depression, eventually finding his way through Christ and back to his father.

We can only imagine when all we will do is forever worship the Lord our God.

Epilogue

The seven letters to the seven churches were complete. But before John could draw another breath he saw directly in front of him an open door and beyond that door a vision which made his heart beat fast in his chest. It was heaven! He remembered what the Lord said to the church in Philadelphia, those who had kept His commands, 'I have placed before you an open door that no-one can shut.' The church age was past and as he moved towards the open door his pulse quickened again as he thought of all the previous visions he had had of heaven. What would it be like? Those mansions Jesus had told them about that He was going to prepare and the Majesty of God His Father.

The voice of his Lord nudged him to the edge of door step, 'Come on, step this way, I want to show you the future. It is all prepared and ready for those who have heard my words and believed them.' Nothing in this world or in his dreams could possibly have prepared him for the sight that greeted him the other side of the door……………………

ACKNOWLEDGEMENTS

It is to the late Burns Shearer that my thanks go for his mentorship encouragement and permission to use his drama of the first chapter. Burns gave of his time, skill as a writer and love to the Scottish Fellowship of Christian Writers whose support I have also enjoyed over many years. To all those who took the time and effort to read the first, second and third drafts I thank enormously, your comments have resulted in this final effort. My prayer partner, Maggie Shearer has followed the progress with her solid commitment and love for me.

My family have given me unconditional love, support, and skilled advice in editing and wise words. They have been the bedrock of my learning in how to behave as wife, mother, mother-in-law, and grandmother. Thank you, David, Emily, Alan, Cameron, Lewis, MaryBeth and Ludo, you are all so precious in His sight. Lastly, but certainly not least, to my mum who is the greatest prayer warrior I know and has consistently prayed over my whole life – thank you for walking beside the journey of my life.

References/Bibliography

Alcorn R 2004 *Heaven* Tyndale Publishers USA

Benware P 1990 *Survey of the New Testament* Revised Edition Moody Press

Bewes, R 2000 ed. *The Lamb Wins A guided tour through the Book of Revelation* Christian focus publications UK

Bishop, J. 1957 *The Day Christ Died* Fontana Publishers.

Bible Journey 2018 Available at: http://www.thebiblejourney.org/biblejourney1/19-johns-letters-to-the-believers-in-asia-minor88730/introduction-to-john-his-3-letters/ accessed 10 April 2018

BaalWorship.2018.Available.at: https://ncfic.org/blog/posts/modern_baal_worship_in_theaters_stadiums_and_living_rooms accessed 24 April 2018

Bible Translations - 1992 Life Application Bible New International Version Kingsway Publishers. The New Living Bible used when quoting the whole letters to the seven churches.

Biblos Maps You are free to use up to 50 Biblos copyrighted maps (small or large) for your website or presentation. Please credit Biblos.com. available at: http://bibleatlas.org accessed 8 June 2018

Christianity Today Available at: http://www.christianitytoday.com/history/people/martyrs/polycarp.html accessed 18 April 2018

Carlson C 1983 *Corrie ten Boom Her Life, Her Faith* Kingsway Publications UK

Expository files on Laodicea 2018 Available at http://www.bible.ca/ef/expository-colossians-4-16.htm accessed 27 April 2018

Gaynor, L. Butterworth, J. 2013 *God's Needle* Monarch publishing Oxford, UK.

Murray, A 2011 *Power in Prayer*. Bethany Publishers USA

Graham Shanks Pastor of Bruntsfield Evangelical Church, Edinburgh, and Ian Naismith: teaching on the letters to the seven churches

Gower, R 1987 *The New Manners, and customs of Bible times* Moody Press Fausset's Bible dictionary

Hansen, C 2004 The Vanishing Act of the church in turkey *Christianity Today* Available at: https://www.christianitytoday.com/history/2008/august/vanishing-act-of-church-in-turkey.html accessed 17 April 18

Hendriksen, W (1973) ed. *More than conquerors: An interpretation of the Book of Revelation* Tyndale Press: London

Holman Hunt Light of the World 2019 Available at: https://commons.wikimedia.org/w/index.php?curid=3400556 accessed 25 May

Lotz, Graham A 1997 *The vision of His Glory* Word Publishing USA

Lennie, T 2015 *Land of Many Revivals* Christian Focus Publications UK

Lewis, C 1958 *The Problem of Pain* Penguin Classics

McCheyne, R. (2001) ed. *The Seven Churches of Asia* Christian Focus Publications: Scotland

McNaughton I (undated) Lord's day in the New Testament Day One Christian Ministries

Milford H 1923 *The Companion Bible* Oxford University Press

Mintz, Z 2015 Available at: http://www.ibtimes.com/first-church-be-built-turkey-nearly-century-1773428 accessed 20 April 2018

Murray, A. 2011 *Power in Prayer* Bethany House Publishers: USA

Morgan C 1952 *Searchlights from the Word* Oliphants Publishers

Morris L 1969 *Revelation – An Introduction and Commentary* London Tyndale Press

Nickens, M 2005 Available at: http://www.studythechurch.com/articles/early-church/polycarp-link accessed 18 April 2018

Open Doors World Watch List 2019 Available at: https://www.opendoorsuk.org/persecution/countries/yemen/ accessed 30 April

Padfield, D 2015 Colossae, Hierapolis and Laodicea Available at: http://www.padfield.com/acrobat/history/laodicea.pdf accessed 27 April 2018

Parkinson, J 2016 *Threads through Revelation* (Front cover) Threads Publishing UK www.revelation-threads.co.uk

Pawson D 2003 *Unlocking the Bible* Second Edition Collins

Pawson, D 2008 *Come with me through Revelation* Terra Nova Publications: UK

Rhodes, R (2013) *40 Days through Revelation: Uncovering the Mystery of the End Times* Harvest House Publishers: USA

Scazzero, P 2017 2nd Ed. *Emotionally Healthy Spirituality* Zondervan USA

Scott E 2007 *Lecture Notes Institute of Biblical Studies* Carrubers Close, Edinburgh

Sherrill, E 2002 *All the Way to Heaven* Eagle Publishing UK

Solomon, M 2018 Available at: http://makingtalmidim.blogspot.co.uk/2016/11/revelation-waking-up-in-sardis-part-one.html accessed 25 April 2018

Stetzer, E 2018 Available at: http://www.christianitytoday.com/edstetzer/2011/june/thursday-is-for-turkey-church-in-smyrna.html accessed 18 April 2018

Still, W. (undated) *And I Saw…. St John's Vision: A Commentary* Didasko Press: Scotland

Stott, J 1986 *The Cross of Christ* 20th anniversary edition Intervarsity Press UK

Strauch, A 2008 *Love or Die: Christ's wake-up call to the Church* Lewis and Roth Publishers USA

Yeoman, S 2018 Medicine in the Ancient World Available at: https://www.biblicalarchaeology.org/daily/ancient-cultures/daily-life-and-practice/medicine-in-the-ancient-world/ Accessed 20 April 2018

Violatti, C. 2015 Pergamum Available at: https://www.ancient.eu/pergamon/ accessed 20 April 2018

ABOUT THE AUTHOR

Ruth Aird is a retired nurse who lives outside Edinburgh with her husband. They have two adult children and two grandchildren. She teaches the Bible to women in small groups in both Scotland and Romania.